RETICULATA

II

Camellias Illustrated

EDITED BY

MORRIE L. SHARP

PUBLICITY COMMITTEE

OREGON CAMELLIA SOCIETY

PORTLAND I, OREGON

To H. H. Harms, whose enthusiasm and zeal have done so much to develop camellia consciousness in the Northwest, and whose constant assistance has been invaluable in preparing this book.

FOREWORD

"Camellias Illustrated" is presented in the hope of furthering the ever increasing interest in and enjoyment of camellias, one of nature's most artistic shrubs and exquisite flowers. The book was underwritten by a group of amateur camellia fanciers and is published under the sponsorship of the Oregon Camellia Society.

The information contained is not based on the experience of any one grower but upon the combined knowledge furnished by outstanding amateur and commercial growers from all sections of the country.

It is our hope that this highly illustrated, complete but concise, and "down-to-earth," popular priced book will extend interest and knowledge among amateurs in all sections of the country and particularly in the "camellia belt."

Experience and knowledge enable any hobbyist to get more pleasure from his endeavor whether he be a collector of artistic pieces, a sportsman or gardener; in the same manner the better informed camellia fancier will be able to raise finer blossoms and get additional pleasure from his hobby.

As with all hobbies and every other endeavor that people try to do well there are differences of opinion in certain phases of camellia culture and various methods may be used to accomplish the same purpose under varying conditions. Hence in the pages devoted to such phases as planting and drainage, several methods that have proven successful under various climatic and soil conditions are mentioned.

Camellias are easy to raise, require a minimum of care, and will give the owner (and even his grandchildren) years of satisfaction if ordinary precautions are taken to see that they are planted in soil and under conditions to their liking and if ordinary care is taken to control pests and disease and to supply food and water during the life of the shrub. Amateurs desiring the finest quality shrubs and blossoms will be well repaid for the slight amount of time spent following the suggestions included in the following pages as they are based on the advice of expert growers from all sections of the country.

We wish to thank the hundreds of expert amateur and professional growers, camellia club officers, garden editors, college and government officials that have assisted us in supplying information to be included in "Camellias Illustrated," also the thousands of camellia enthusiasts who have expressed their interest, and the prominent photographers, both professional and amateur, mentioned on the following page, who have supplied many of the illustrations used.

Again our only hope is that this book will further the interest in and enjoyment of camellias.

APPRECIATION

We wish to thank the many people who have given so freely of their time, knowledge and advice to assist in the preparation of "Camellias Illustrated."

Special thanks is due R. J. Wilmot, Secretary of the American Camellia Society; H. H. Harms and Clyde P. Bradley, Past Presidents of the Oregon Camellia Society; Robert F. Hamilton, President of the Oregon Camellia Society; Dean Collins, Garden Editor of the Oregon Journal, Carl Maskey, Garden Advisor and Field Representative for the Oregon Journal and C. S. Weisenberg, Art Director, for their continual assistance.

Also to the following contributors of articles: Lord Aberconway, Royal Horticultural Society, London, "Camellias and Camellia Culture in Great Britain;" A. E. Morrison, "Plant Diseases and Insect Pests of Camellias;" Mrs. R. F. Hamilton, "Camellia Corsages;" Mrs. H. W. Van Hoy, "Camellias in Arrangements;" Dr. V. T. Stoutemyer, Dr. Walter E. Lammerts, B. Y. Morrison and C. F. Kinman for information included in the article on "Wintering Camellias in Cold Climates;" and Harold H. Sherley for supplying the "Pronunciation Guide."

Appreciation is also expressed to Mrs. H. H. Harms, C. E. Stephens, Dr. Clement G. Bowers, Earl R. Norgard, Charles Vollum, Donald P. Abbott, as well as Miss Louise Weick, Rolly Langley, Cecil Solly and other Garden Editors, and the many commercial camellia growers from all sections of the country for their advice and assistance.

Many of the fine illustrations were supplied through the courtesy of J. G. Bacher, a well known garden lecturer and amateur photographer, and Glenn L. McDowell, amateur photographer, both of Portland; and the Oregon Journal and Al Monner and Les Ordeman, Journal staff photographers. Other photographs and illustrations were supplied by A. E. Morrison, Dr. T. H. Goodspeed, H. M. Davis, Oregon State College Extension Service, Alabama Agricultural Experiment Station, J. O. Lambert, Florida News and Photo Service, Inc., Cranford Miniatures, E. R. Gschwind, Lawrence T. Mayer and K. Sawada.

Other photographs and colored illustrations were furnished by O. E. Hopfer of Oakland, California, founder and first president of the Northern California Camellia Society and well known for his many magazine articles on camellias. His chief interest is in propagating and hybridizing camellias.

Also by Robert F. and Eloise Hamilton, members of the Oregon Camellia Society and prominent local photographers specializing in garden and color photography and Edward Ferrill, amateur photographer of Salem, Oregon, a member of both the Oregon Camellia and Salem Camellia and Rhododendron Societies.

Reference is made to "Camellias in America" by Dr. H. Harold Hume; "Azaleas and Camellias for the Garden" by Ben Arthur Davis, Garden Editor, Holland's Magazine; and the Oregon Camellia Society Annual, "Camellias As a Hobby."

Valuable information pertaining to propagation was obtained from the U. S. Department of Agriculture Bulletin on "Propagation of Trees and Shrubs" by Guy E. Yerkes and the Oregon State College Extension Service Bulletin on "Grafting and Budding" by Professor W. P. Duruz.

CONTENTS

LIST OF COLOR ILLUSTRATIONS

DEBUTANTE

ELENA NOBILE

BLACK PRINCE

FRED SANDER*

MATHOTIANA

*Bloom illustrated is known as *Fimbriata Superba* (a sport of Fred Sander) in the Pacific
Northwest.

11

RETICULATA

CAMELLIA HISTORY

Camellias, so popular with gardeners in many parts of the world today, are direct descendants or improved varieties of the species plants that have grown in Eastern Asia for centuries.

More than 200 years ago European traders, particularly those of the British East India Company, discovered these plants growing wild in China, Japan and the islands along the Asiatic coast line. Their beauty led to the importation of seed as well as plants into the British Isles and other parts of Europe.

In the interesting chapters devoted to camellia history in "Camellias in America" Dr. H. H. Hume states that an article published by G. E. Edwards in 1745 included an illustration of a camellia but referred to it as a Chinese Rose. The name camellia was later given in honor of George Joseph Kamel, Society of Jesus Missionary.

CAMELLIAS IN AMERICA

Camellias were first introduced in America a little over 150 years ago. Through the development of seedlings and importations many varieties were grown in southern gardens by the time of the Civil War.

Another interesting book "Azaleas and Camellias for the Garden" by Ben Arthur Davis, Garden Editor of Holland's Magazine, contains the following paragraphs.

"We do not know when or how the camellia was introduced in our Southern home grounds, but we do know that travelers in the early years of the settlement of the South brought plants with them from the 'Old Country,' and very early in the development of the country specimens of *Camellia japonica* were found in the vicinity of Charleston, Augusta, Pensacola, Mobile, New Orleans, Natchez, and other centers of wealth and culture. The records indicate that long before the Civil War there were more than 100 varieties of camellias grown in the Magnolia Gardens near Charleston, and no doubt there were many other old plantings in the South which contained a considerable number of varieties during this period.

"Many of these old plants are yet growing vigorously in their original locations, while numbers of others have been collected and replanted in some of the most pretentious public and private gardens. Flowers from many of these old plants were given friends, the stems rooted, mostly in shady spots with glass jars turned over them, and thus the varieties increased."

The earliest plantings on the Pacific Coast that have come to our attention were made in the vicinity of Sacramento, California about 1860. Many of these are still living and blooming profusely each year, even those that received little or no care. Descriptions and an illustration of these plantings are included on page 104.

PRESENT POPULARITY

Interest in camellias slackened in the late 19th and early 20th century. However the beauty of their evergreen foliage and early bloom brought about a revival of interest and few if any shrubs have ever enjoyed such an increase of popularity as have camellias during the past few years.

Naturally this revival of interest has been partially due to the many fine new varieties developed by commercial growers during recent years (according to advice received from many prominent growers, gardeners have some real additional treats in store when some of the fine new varieties already developed are propagated in sufficient quantity to permit open market distribution).

Proof of the ever-increasing interest in this beautiful, aristocratic shrub comes from all parts of the country. A few examples are mentioned below. Pensacola, Florida, Greensville, Alabama, Coos Bay, Oregon, Sacramento, and Temple City, California have officially adopted the slogan "Camellia City" and advice from these areas indicates that current plantings warrant the slogan.

A camellia queen annually presides over the Jacksonville, Florida show. Illustrated is Miss Mary McGee, Queen, fittingly wearing a crown of camellias (photo courtesy of Florida News and Photograph Service).

Many leading hotels are establishing camellia rooms, including Camellia House dining room in the Drake, Chicago, Illinois.

New Orleans, Louisiana, has a floral trail featuring camellias and azaleas.

Garden Editors from all parts of the country advise of increased popularity. Particularly interesting are the reports from Garden

CAMELLIA QUEEN

14

Editors located in the colder parts of the country that interest is increasing in both the cut flower markets and from a cultural standpoint. Amateurs in these colder climates, including many without greenhouses, are devising means of winter protection which enable them to raise camellias.

The remark of a San Francisco Garden Editor exemplifies those received from sections that are normally considered in the "camellia belt." This editor advised that interest is at an all time high and that fully 90% of the new homes built in the better residential sections are featuring camellia plantings in their landscaping.

SPECIES OF CAMELLIAS

The exact number of species or types of camellias is not accurately known. Experts estimate that anywhere from less than a dozen to 30 or 40 species exist.

For purposes of this book four species will be considered, as practically all camellias of interest to American amateur growers will fall within one of these groups. They are *C. japonica, C. Sasanqua, C. reticulata and C. saluenensis.*

Camellia japonica

C. japonica is beyond all doubt the most popular species in America.

The amateur gardener may select from several hundred varieties of this species ranging in colors from white to many shades of pink and red, including a wide assortment of variegated colors.

Bloom forms range from singles to semi-doubles to doubles. Most *japonica* blossoms are scentless, however a few are fragrant, particularly when the blossom has been open several days.

The various varieties feature evergreen foliage ranging in shape from long narrow leaves to almost round. Further information pertaining to the leaves will be more thoroughly discussed later.

In many areas of the Pacific Coast section of the "camellia belt" *C. japonica* differs from some other species and from many other shrubs in that it has two cycles of new growth per year. The time of these cycles naturally varies according to the climate and section of the country. The first appears shortly after the blooming period and the second about four to six months later.

C. Sasanqua

The second most popular species in this country, if popularity is based on the number of varieties grown by amateurs, is *Camellia Sasanqua.*

The majority of the named varieties are of single bloom form, ranging in color from white to red. A few named varieties feature variegated bloom as well as double blossom forms.

15

KUMASAKA

16

Sasanquas are hardier than *japonicas* and may be grown in colder climates without protection in winter.

This species is gaining in popularity and being added to the collections of many amateur growers because of the earliness of bloom. Most varieties bloom several months ahead of the average *japonica* and at a time when few other flowers are available in the average garden.

Another feature of interest is that most *Sasanquas* are fragrant.

Since they are considered fast growers they are recommended for hedge treatment and open growth often leads to espalier adaptations.

C. reticulata

C. reticulata, which at present is proving so popular in many parts of this country, particularly on the Pacific Coast, is really a very old species, having been grown and proven popular in England since the early 1800's.

C. reticulata is a more tender plant than either *japonica* or *Sasanqua*. As it will not stand colder climates, it is considered a greenhouse species in many sections of the "camellia belt," including the Pacific Northwest, where it differs from *japonicas* in that it has one cycle of growth per year and in that the plant is rangy and not bushy.

C. reticulata produces few lateral buds, hence growth is practically all terminal. If the terminal bud is removed, adventitious buds along the branch seldom form and growth stops.

The leaves are very unusual in that they are thick, flat and a very dull green. They are usually long and narrow with prominent dark veins and serrated edges.

The semi-double blooms are often six to eight inches in size and feature large ruffled petals. *C. reticulata* has proven harder to propagate from cuttings though not too difficult to graft.

The semi-double garden form is the type of the species but the wild, single form has been discovered and is also available now.

C. saluenensis

While *C. saluenensis* is not found in the average garden it does deserve the consideration of camellia enthusiasts, particularly those interested in hybridizing and developing new varieties from seed.

Experiments to date indicate that crossing *saluenensis* with *japonica* tends toward fragrant blossoms and hardier plants.

Saluenensis has been in this country for some time but its varieties were mistakenly classed as *japonicas* or *Sasanquas*. Recent studies have shown that there are several varieties among Japanese imports that have not been heretofore recognized as *saluenensis*.

The fragrance of *saluenensis* is much clearer than that of *Sansanqua* which has a more or less spicy or musky under-odor.

17

Top—TRICOLOR RED and a white sport on same bush.

Center—JARVIS RED.

Lower—CAMELLIA HEDGE—Section of the informal 15-year old camellia hedge at the rear of Mr. and Mrs. William J. Lyon's gardens, Portland, Oregon.

CAMELLIAS IN LANDSCAPING

Entirely aside from the "satisfaction" given each year in the form of one of nature's most beautiful blossoms, camellias would probably increase in popularity due alone to their adaptability in landscaping and beautifying the lawn.

Their pleasing shape and habit of growth together with the dark green, rich and luxurious evergreen foliage make them equally at home in the formal garden or the most informal planting.

Depending on individual taste they may be used as a background for perennial and annual borders and beds or as points of accent for driveway or entrances. Varieties and species may be selected that offer rangy, loose growth or others that feature compact symmetrical branches.

Regardless of the way camellias are used in landscaping they should be allowed ample space. As they have a long life expectancy and over a period of years will grow to become large shrubs and even trees it is necessary to allow ample growing space or later remove adjoining shrubs that would crowd the camellias. This growing space not only assists in developing a beautiful symmetrical shrub but is beneficial in allowing plenty of air and circulation which tends to prevent disease and is of help in controlling pests.

CAMELLIAS AS A HEDGE

Many gardeners are using camellias for new hedges or to replace old ones. Depending on individual taste these hedge plantings may be of one variety and color or an assortment of varieties, both as to color and blooming season as well as foliage.

The single variety hedge is often considered more pleasing and naturally more formal during the blooming period. But growers wishing to have a wide selection in their collection and without sufficient space to accommodate such an assortment may prefer to plant an assorted variety camellia hedge. For a permanent hedge camellias should be planted at least four or five feet apart. Gardeners desiring quicker results may prefer to place the plants closer together and later remove or transplant every other one, should they become too crowded.

To insure a dense, low, bushy growth camellias used in hedges may require more thorough pruning than those used for other purposes. As the plants become larger the amount of pruning in later years will depend on whether a symmetrical or informal type of hedge is desired.

Rapid growing bushy varieties are usually selected for hedge plantings. Because of their rapid growth many hedge plantings feature certain varieties of *Sasanquas*.

Certain loose growing varieties of *Sasanquas* as well as *japonicas* lend themselves to espalier treatment. This use calls for training the branches laterally to wires, trellises, or the side of the building as shown in the illustration.

If properly trained and pruned, this type of growth will be a highlight of the garden the year around and a sight not soon to be forgotten when in bloom.

CAMELLIA HEDGE

The camellia hedge illustrated above borders the driveway entrance to the home of H. M. Davis, El Monte, California. The hedge is kept trimmed to a height of 36 inches and consists of 5-year old Covina Red Camellias which were planted 18 inches apart. Mr. Davis advises that the hedge requires much less care than a privet or box wood hedge and gives the added pleasure of color in the garden and an abundance of cut flowers for the house during the blooming season.

"CAMELLIA BELT"

As the majority of camellias grown outdoors in America today prefer climates without too severe winters, the largest plantings are in the Southern and Pacific Coast states as indicated on the map on page 22. Many growers have felt that a high humidity was also required but camellias have been very successfully grown in and around such areas as Sacramento, California, where the average summer humidity is only about forty and often drops into the lower twenties. Naturally, camellias grown in such areas require plenty of water during the entire growing season, including the fall months.

As soil and climatic conditions vary even in adjoining towns, all areas in the states indicated do not offer ideal growing conditions; however, camellias may be grown outdoors in most parts of this area (except cold mountainous regions, etc.), providing proper soil, drainage, and sufficient water are provided.

Growers have advised that cold spells as low as two degrees above zero have caused no permanent damage to plants, although buds are often injured.

Rapid changes in temperature, such as cold nights followed by warm sunny days have been known to cause some damage including occasional splitting of the bark.

A prominent amateur grower feels that plants stand extremely cold spells much better when the soil is moist at the time of the freeze. He attributes this to the fact that freezing is a drying process.

In the hopes of enabling gardeners living in the more extreme climates and without a greenhouse at their disposal to enjoy camellias, extensive correspondence has been carried on with many experts and many helpful suggestions have been received. Nurserymen state they have many customers living in areas that were formerly considered too cold for camellias. They usually recommend single and semi-double varieties as experiments have shown that they stand the cold better. Some commercial men also recommend that established plants which have been grafted on sturdy root stocks be planted in these areas.

Another suggestion is that early or late varieties which bloom before or after the normal period of cold weather in a particular area be selected.

Among the *japonicas* suggested for colder sections are Lady Vansittart, Lady Vansittart Red, Jarvis Red, Semi-Double Blush, T. K. Variegated, Tricolor (Red and Siebold), Donckelari, Daikagura, Kumasaka (plain and variegated), Lady Clare, and Ethrington White. Most varieties of *Sasanquas* have proven their ability to withstand winters in areas too cold for unprotected outdoor culture of *japonicas*.

In areas where winters are not too severe, sufficient protection is often afforded by covering the plant with burlap during cold spells and removing it when the temperature rises. This or some other method of shading also helps prevent too rapid a thawing process after cold spells. As previously mentioned, rapid thawing is often more harmful than the cold spell itself.

In extremely cold sections, many growers have been raising camellias in pots or wooden tubs and moving them indoors or affording other means of protection during the winter.

Another proof that interest in camellia culture is no longer confined to any particular section is that inquiries for "Camellias as a Hobby," the annual published by the Oregon Camellia Society, have been received from every state as well as several foreign countries. A paragraph devoted to the book that appeared in the July issue of "House and Garden" has to date resulted in correspondence from 39 states, the District of Columbia, Hawaii, Canada, the Panama Canal Zone, Australia, and England.

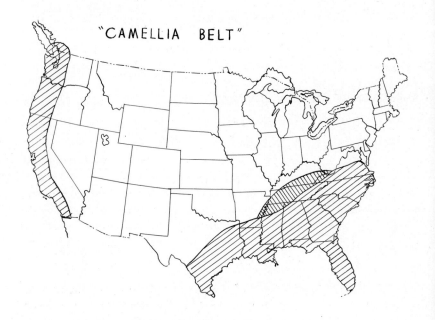

"CAMELLIA BELT"

The above map indicates the approximate area where year around outdoor culture of camellias has been successful. Both *japonicas* and *Sasanquas* are grown in most of the area along the Pacific Coast and the Southern and Gulf States that is shaded in the more horizontal manner on the map. *Sasanquas*, usually more hardy, are grown outdoors in colder areas such as that indicated by the more vertical shading and in other regions along the Atlantic Seaboard and further inland in the Pacific Northwest. As climatic and soil conditions vary even in adjoining cities no map can furnish a completely accurate picture. Growers are continually reporting successful outdoor culture in other colder areas when some winter protection is provided.

PLANTING CAMELLIAS

Too much emphasis cannot be placed on the importance of taking proper precautions when planting camellias. The short period of time required to provide the desired growing conditions will be well repaid by healthier plants and more beautiful profuse blooms.

Basically camellias require good drainage, proper soil, adequate light and space. When these are provided at the time of planting only ordinary care such as watering, fertilizing, so forth will be necessary in later years to assure the maximum beauty of both flower and foliage.

PLANTING OR TRANSPLANTING

In most areas small camellias may be planted during any period of the year except in extremely hot or cold months.

Larger camellias may be planted or transplanted during the months of January, February, March, October, November and December in practically all areas. In milder climates they may often be planted in April and September as well.

Camellias purchased from reliable growers are ready to plant when obtained. However in transplanting camellias in your own lawn it is advisable that large plants be root pruned before moving. This should be done several months in advance of moving.

ROOT PRUNE

To root prune a plant a sharp spade is forced down full depth around it in a vertical position and at such distance from the plant's trunk as to form a circle whose diameter is not less than one fourth of the plant's height. Root pruning cuts off the large roots so that during the following months a mass of small fibrous roots grow out of the remaining portion of the large roots, providing the plant with an adequate root system to feed it during the time that it is re-establishing itself in the new location.

LOCATION

As camellias generally serve as the permanent shrubbery background for an attractive yard and consequently are seldom moved, due consideration should be given to the matter of adequate growing space and to their place in the yard's area.

SUN OR SHADE

The question as to whether camellias should be planted in full sun or partial shade varies according to the climatic conditions and to the variety to be planted.

23

FULL SUN   PARTIAL SHADE

In areas with mild cool summers, all but the most delicate colored varieties may be planted in full sun. In these areas camellias which have been planted in sunny locations generally produce more flowers, are bushier, and better withstand attacks of diseases and pests than those which have been planted in shady locations. Those which have been planted in shady locations usually hold the color of their flowers and foliage over a longer period of time.

Even in cooler climates precautions should be taken against reflected sun. Camellias should not be planted close to concrete or white walls that reflect afternoon sun.

In a warmer section of the country camellias should receive protection from the hot mid-day and afternoon sun. This shade may be provided naturally by trees or buildings or artificially by lath-house or other means. Full shade during the entire day should be avoided.

Regardless of climatic conditions protection from strong winds will assure longer lasting and more beautiful bloom.

Providing good drainage is an absolute must in planting camellias. They require sufficient moisture at all times but will not survive in soil that is water logged during rainy seasons.

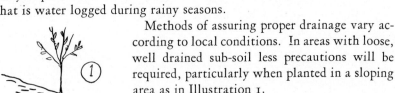

Methods of assuring proper drainage vary according to local conditions. In areas with loose, well drained sub-soil less precautions will be required, particularly when planted in a sloping area as in Illustration 1.

As this ideal condition does not exist in most areas many prominent commercial growers recommend that camellias be planted as shown in Illustration 2. This method

24

of providing drainage should prove adequate except in areas with heavy sub-soil that will not absorb the moisture drained off by the gravel.

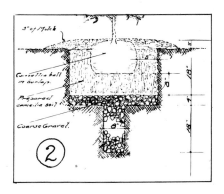

In areas with heavy sub-soil, commercial growers as well as amateurs often recommend that drainage tile be laid that will carry off the water. It is well to remember that the laying of drainage tile, as shown in Illustration 3, will not only benefit camellias but the lawn and other flowers and ornamental shrubs as well.

Another method that often solves the drainage problem is to build a raised section in the garden using good sandy friable soil and planting camellias in this raised portion.

DRAINAGE TILE

Regardless of method, adequate drainage is essential for healthy profuse blooming plants.

SOIL

Like most flowers and shrubs, camellias require a fertile loose soil condition. In addition they require soil with an acid reaction as do azaleas, rhododendrons and mountain-laurel.

When the acidity of the soil is not known it is advisable that it be tested before planting camellias. This may be done with one of the inexpensive soil kits sold by seed stores or in many areas by sending a sample of the soil to a County Agricultural Agent or State College for testing.

The symbol used to express the acid or alkaline condition of the soil is pH. Camellias prefer a pH of between 5 and 6 (7 is neutral, below 7 acid, and above 7 alkaline).

If soil is not acid enough the condition may be improved by adding aluminum sulphate or sulphur. Sulphur is somewhat slower in action but is preferred by many growers. Usually one or two pounds per hundred square feet of soil is sufficient. However some soils with a high pH require 3 or 4 pounds of sulphur.

In areas where soil shows a high alkaline reaction camellias are being successfully grown in containers or by using the following method.

Drainage tile is laid approximately 30 inches under the soil level to carry off surface and underground water. The alkaline soil is removed from an area at least 3 or 4 feet square and to the depth of the drainage tile. This hole is then filled with the proper acid type soil.

Should your soil be too acid (a pH of below 4½ or 5) the condition may be corrected by "sweetening" the soil with lime.

In most areas once the proper acid condition is obtained it can usually be maintained in future years by an occasional but regular light applications of sulphur or by using acid type fertilizer.

Should you live in an area with alkaline soil or with an alkaline water supply more attention will be required. Advice from a New Orleans commercial grower states that the water supply there is alkaline. This grower suggests the following method of maintaining an acid soil reaction in his area.

"Acidity can be taken care of very easily in New Orleans where the city water supply is alkaline by dissolving to every gallon of water one tablespoon of aluminum sulphate and watering the base of the plant with this solution every three or four months. In this soluble form the acid reaction is immediate and is uniform in strength over the area watered."

PREPARATION OF SOIL

In addition to requiring acid and a well drained soil, camellias and most other shrubs, prefer a humus fertile soil. How this condition is obtained will largely depend on the condition of the soil where the camellia is to be planted and on the preference of the particular grower. As shown in Illustration 4 the hole for the camellia should be dug large enough to allow at least 8 or 10 inches of "camellia soil" on all sides and under the ball of the plant. When the illustrated gravel drainage method is to be

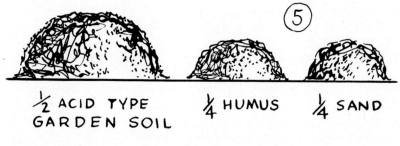

½ ACID TYPE GARDEN SOIL   ¼ HUMUS   ¼ SAND

+ FERTILIZER = "CAMELLIA SOIL"

used the hole should be deep enough to allow at least 8 inches of soil plus a minimum of 4 inches of gravel. As shown an additional hole at least 18 inches deep is dug in the center and filled with gravel (a post hole digger will be convenient for digging the smaller hole).

If the soil removed was alkaline or of poor quality it should be disposed of and good "camellia soil" substituted.

CAMELLIA SOIL

An excellent soil mixture for planting camellias consists of ½ good acid type soil, ¼ humus which may be in the form of leaf mold, peat moss, Redwood Bark Mulch, or decomposed sawdust, plus ¼ sharp sand. (See Illustration 5.) A liberal quantity of well rotted barnyard fertilizer may be mixed with this soil or from one to three or four handfuls of cottonseed meal or commercial fertilizer (the amount depending on the size of the plant).

When fast acting commercial fertilizers are used it is advisable to mix the soil preparation well in advance of planting or see that the fertilizer does not come in direct contact with the roots.

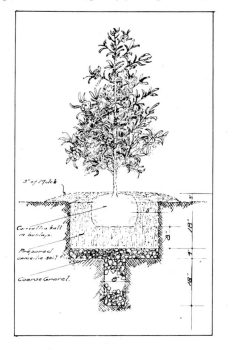

PLANTING

The main essential to remember when actually planting a camellia is that they are "surface feeders" and must not be planted deep. The crown of the

ILLUSTRATION 4

root ball should never be below the level of the surrounding soil.

Most growers recommend that enough soil be firmly tamped in the bottom of the hole to allow the top of the root ball to be about 2 inches above the level of the adjacent ground at the time of planting. This is an added drainage precaution and should also assure the ball remaining at or slightly above ground level in case of future settling in cases where the soil was not firmly packed.

Growers in some sections of the South recommend filling the hole to a depth that will allow most of the root ball to rest above ground level and then adding soil adjacent to the ball and to the level of the top of the crown as shown in Illustration 6. The outer edge of this mound is raised to a slightly higher level forming a "cup" for easier watering.

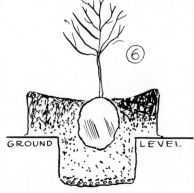

Regardless of planting level recommended by growers in your area the crown of the ball should not be covered with soil and all soil below and at the sides should be firmly packed to prevent air pockets.

The plant should be thoroughly soaked at the time of planting and many growers, particularly those in warmer climates, suggest adding a layer of mulch to help hold moisture.

Camellia hedge owned by
Mrs. Sheffield Phelps,
Aiken, S. C.

Left—*Sasanqua* Cleopatra.

HERME

ECSTASY

Lady Vansittart Red

Latifolia Red

Carolyn S.

Te Deum

31

MAGNOLIAEFLORA

CAMELLIA CULTURE

Providing camellias have been properly planted and ordinary precautions are taken to prevent disease and pests (as adequately covered elsewhere) the only future care usually required is proper watering, fertilizing, pruning, and mulching.

SOAK ROOT BALL

Probably the most essential of these is watering as this not only assures proper growth and development of flower buds but is a definite aid in the prevention of disease.

Camellias prefer a moist soil condition at all times. Just how often they should be watered during the summer and early fall months will depend on climatic and soil conditions. In most instances a thorough soaking of the root ball once every week or so should suffice. Water should be supplied in sufficient quantity to allow its penetration to the deepest roots.

SPRINKLE FOLIAGE

In addition to soaking the soil the foliage should be sprinkled at more frequent intervals. This watering of the foliage is helpful in the prevention of pests as well as beneficial to the foliage and plant during hot spells.

The foliage sprinkling does not replace the necessity of soaking the soil, however and should not be done while direct sun rays are on plant.

FERTILIZING

Fertilizers are applied to develop plant growth and assist in maintaining a healthy camellia as well as develop and "set" the following season's buds. Many varieties of camellias bloom so profusely that the plant is left in a somewhat weakened condition at the end of the flowering period.

Many old-time growers believe that the most important time to apply fertilizer is right after the blooming season, or before blooming for the late blooming varieties. These same experienced growers feel, however, that more camellias have been injured by overfertilizing than by applying too little. They emphasize that the principle reason for fertilizing in most soils is to replace the plant food taken out by the camellia in developing its growth and blooms.

The amount of chemical fertilizer will vary according to the size of the plant and the condition of the soil. Under most soil conditions a cupful is plenty for the average five foot plant and no more than a small handful need be given younger bushes. If commercial fertilizers are used they should be evenly scattered in a circle around the root ball as illustrated and thoroughly soaked into the soil to prevent burning the surface roots.

Most varieties of camellias start new growth and form new buds at the end of the blooming season or shortly thereafter. Hence fertilizer applied at this time is beneficial.

Growers also recommend another light application of fertilizer later. This is usually done in June in areas where camellias bloom early and a month or so later in sections where the peak blooming season is later.

An application of barnyard fertilizer or cottonseed meal in the fall is also often recommended. When this is done less chemical fertilizer is required the next year.

As mentioned under planting, camellias require an acid type soil, hence one of the acid type camellia or azalea fertilizers or a light application of sulphur or aluminum sulphate applied at the same time as a regular fertilizer is advisable on soils without sufficient acidity.

MULCHING

Mulches are placed at the roots of camellias to help maintain a cooler soil condition during hot months, to retain the moisture in the soil, and in the case of acid type mulches, such as peat moss, pine needles, Redwood Bark Mulch, oak leaves, so forth, to assist in maintaining an acid soil condition. The thickness of the required mulch varies according to the type of material used. Thinner applications should be made of materials that have a tendency to pack.

Mulches should not be applied, or allowed to accumulate over a period of years, to a depth that will be injurious to the root ball. This would prove as detrimental as planting too deeply.

Some mulches serve as a source of plant food as they decay. The amount of food substance supplied varies according to the mulch used. Vegetable matter such as leaf mold and grass cuttings supply considerable but peat moss little or none.

When heavy mulches are applied it is often desirable to use a high nitrogen content fertilizer to replace the nitrogen taken from the soil in decomposing the mulch.

Top
MONJISU RED

Lower
AMABILIS

35

PRUNING CAMELLIAS

Many camellia growers place too little importance on pruning. Probably because of fear of losing the following season's bloom, they often confine their pruning to the removal of occasional dead, diseased, or leggy branches that mar the appearance of the shrub.

Observing and experienced growers will prune more drastically, particularly their older camellias, to assure more vigorous plants. This will in turn cause healthier shrubs less likely to be attacked by diseases and pests, and also finer blossoms.

In addition to removing any dead branches close to the trunk and the lower, droopy ones, and trimming outer branches to shape the plant, the inner branches should be thinned. This is particularly true in areas where pests and diseases are prevalent as it allows better ventilation and reduces danger of attack. The dense inner-branches seldom produce large flowers or sturdy new growth.

Camellias may be pruned at any time of the year. However, if the heavier pruning is done before new buds and growth forms, it will have less effect on the following season's bloom.

As small camellias do not have a dense center growth, less drastic pruning is required. They will develop into well shaped plants sooner if the ends of several of the branches are trimmed so that the lateral buds will develop into new branches.

C. reticulata is an exception to this rule. Few lateral buds are produced by *reticulata* so that it is natural for the plant's growth to be rangy. If the terminal buds of this species are removed adventitious buds along the branch seldom form and growth is likely to stop.

In all pruning only sharp tools should be used to avoid bruising the bark or branch.

DISBUDDING AND CULTIVATING

Most varieties of camellias "set" so many buds that growers who prefer fewer but larger blooms advise disbudding the plants. To be effective disbudding should be done several months prior to the blooming season so that the remaining buds will receive more nourishment.

A longer blooming season will be assured if when disbudding some of the small buds are removed and not just the larger ones.

Any extensive cultivation should be avoided near camellia plants because when properly planted their roots are near the surface of the soil. Weeds may be pulled out or can usually be avoided by applying mulches.

(Since writing the above, we have read and recommend the article "Sharpen Up Those Rusty Shears" by Mr. C. Norwood Hastie, Jr., which appeared in the 1947 American Camellia Society Annual.—ED's NOTE.)

Top
APPLE BLOSSOM
(*saluenensis* species)

Center
GRANDIFLORA ALBA buds—
probably has largest buds of any
camellia variety.

Lower
ELIZABETH ARDEN

37

GREENHOUSE CULTURE

In cold or rainy climates, the camellia enthusiast who owns a greenhouse large enough to permit under glass culture of camellias is indeed fortunate. Even when no attempt is made to force the plants he will usually enjoy large, beautiful blossoms several weeks ahead of his less fortunate neighbor.

In wet climates the glass will protect the more delicate colored varieties from rain which has a tendency to discolor the bloom, particularly on smaller plants whose foliage and size afford little protection for the blossom. This bloom discoloration (not to be confused with blossom blight disease) is not caused by the rain itself but by the warm sun shining on the flower while it is still covered with raindrops thereby causing it to burn.

Camellias grown under glass require the same well drained, friable, acid type, fertile soil as those grown in the open. Some growers plant them in tubs while others prefer to plant directly in the ground. When permanently planted in this manner, sufficient growing space should be allowed for future development as plants grown under glass usually show more rapid growth.

In milder climates the glass itself may furnish all of the protection necessary but in colder climates arrangements for maintaining a temperature of 35° to 40° at night and slightly higher during the day should be provided. Higher temperatures are required to force blooms.

During hot sunny days the camellias should be protected from the direct sun. That is usually accomplished by applying whitewash on the glass. Plenty of ventilation, frequent spraying of the foliage with the hose to maintain a damp cool atmosphere, and sufficient moisture in the soil are also required.

The same procedure of fertilizing and mulching as followed on plants grown outside should be followed, except that the first application of fertilizer should be made earlier because of the advanced blooming period. Due to more rapid and profuse growth many growers prune and disbud greenhouse plants a little more heavily.

Commercial growers, raising cut flowers for the floral trade, favor such varieties as Alba Plena, Elegans (Chandler), Herme, Frau Minna Seidel, Pope Pius IX, Prof. C. S. Sargent, Mathotiana Alba, Glen 40, Magnoliaeflora, C. M. Hovey, Daikagura, Debutante, Lallarook, Mathotiana, Pink Ball and Purity for greenhouse culture.

H. H. Harms inspects his greenhouse filled with choice camellias.

Center
Mrs. Bertha A. Harms
See page 62 for details.

Lower
Shriners' Hospital for Crippled Children, where Oregon Camellia Society is sponsoring camellia plantings.

(*Journal Helicopter photo*)

CAMELLIAS AND CAMELLIA CULTURE
IN GREAT BRITAIN

At the suggestion of Mr. Edmund de Rothschild correspondence was carried on with Lord Aberconway, Head of the Royal Horticultural Society, regarding camellia culture in England.

We are indeed indebted to Lord Aberconway and the Royal Horticultural Society for the following report on camellias in the British Isles.

Our original intention was to rewrite the material into a chapter for "CAMELLIAS ILLUSTRATED." *However we feel that American camellia growers will find Lord Aberconway's letter so interesting that it is reprinted with only a few minor deletions.*—EDITOR'S NOTE.

Thank you very much for your letter of May 29. I was very much interested to hear of the Camellia book which you are publishing.

In regard to the various technical points on which you require information I enclose, as Appendix A, a list of the more popular varieties grown in England.

Camellias are remarkably free from disease in Great Britain, and apparently are subject to only one disease which attacks the leaves and is here described:

CAMELLIA LEAF BLOTCH (*Pestalozzia Guepini*)

Found on Camellia, Rhododendron and Magnolia. On mature plants usually only a few leaves can be found with the blotches, never doing much damage to the plants. The disease can be serious on cuttings and young plants of Camellia and Magnolia under glass, owing to the destruction of a good deal of the leaf surfaces.

The symptoms are blotches on the leaves, in general rounded in shape, bleached to a silvery-white colour on the upper surface, with a strongly defined margin and sprinkled with very small black dots which are pustules of spores. The spores are somewhat spindle-shaped, with three or four transverse divisions, the middle cells being brown and the top and bottom cells colourless. These end cells are attenuated towards each end and the apical cell bears a tuft of three or four long, colourless hairs like a crest. The spore length is about 20.

Our remedy is to cut off infected leaves, or, in young plants even parts of leaves, and follow by spraying with a copper-containing spray such as colloidal copper.

The chief pests are Scale Insects, more especially the Soft Scale, *Lecanium hesperidum*, which is widely distributed on plants grown under glass. It occurs, also, on plants grown outdoors in the Southwestern districts of England, including Cornwall, Devon, Dorset and in the Scilly Isles. This Scale may persist on plants grown in sheltered situations in the Home and Southern Counties of England.

Mealy Bugs, *Pseudococcus species*, are abundantly found on plants grown under glass.

The most effective insecticide is a White Oil and Nicotine emulsion applied forcefully to both surfaces of the foliage and shoots.

The peak blooming season in this country for *japonicas* is in April.

There are, as far as I know, no camellia shows held in England, nor are there any camellia clubs or societies.

In regard to your request for photographs, I have asked the Secretary of the Royal Horticultural Society to see if he can obtain any such pictures and forward them to you in due course. (See page 43 for photographs.)

With reference to your question as to whether the colour of grafted camellia blooms is affected by the root-stock, one of the Society's experts on this subject has contributed the following paragraph:

"It is theoretically possible that the colour of the flowers of a grafted camellia might be affected by the stock if the rate of intake of certain substances by the roots of the stock was different from that of the scion and if the substances concerned had an influence on flower colour, but we have no evidence of such an effect in this country, and we think it extremely unlikely that it would take place."

Signed
ABERCONWAY

POPULAR CAMELLIAS GROWN IN BRITAIN

(1) SPECIES

C. saluenensis —

C. reticulata (wild form) — single: rose-pink.

C. reticulata (garden form) — semi-double: deep rose-pink.

C. oleifolia — (sweet-scented), single: white, pink in bud. This Camellia may be a form of *C. Sasanqua*.

C. Sasanqua — single, early flowering: white, pink and red forms.

C. cuspidata — single, late: small white flowers.

C. maliflora — double: pink.

C. japonica — single: deep red.

You will note that Latinized varietal names are not capitalized and are in italics. This is the correct usage, but in America varietal names are Anglicized and capitalized. *C. oleifolia* referred to is known in America as *C. oleifera*.—EDITOR'S NOTE.

x Camellia J. C. Williams — single: pale pink.
x Camellia Mary Christian — single: pink.
alba plena — double: white.
Adolph Audusson — semi-double: bright crimson.
alba simplex — single: white.
Apple blossom — single: white slightly pink.
Apollo — semi-double: red.
Arejishii — semi-double: deep red.
Campbellii — semi-double: rose pink.
Chandler's elegans — semi-double: light rose often mottled with white.
Compton's Brow — single: white.
Compton's Brow — single: pink.
x Cornish Snow* — single; white, occasional pink flush.
Countess of Orkney — double: white striped pink.
De la Reine — double: white striped deep pink.
Donkelaari — semi-double: deep red.
Fred Sander — double: cerise red.
Gloire de Nantes — semi-double: rose pink.
imbricata rubra — semi-double: cerise maroon.
Jupiter — single: red.
Joy Sander — single: light pink.
Lady Clare — semi-double: rose pink.
latifolia — semi-double: deep red.
magnoliaeflora — semi-double: shell pink.
magnoliaeflora alba — semi-double: white.
Mathottiana — double: deep red.
Mathottiana alba — double: white.
Mars — semi-double: rich crimson.
Mercury — double: bright red.
nobilissima — double: white.
Preston Rose — imbricated double: rose.
Salutation** — single or semi-double; delicate pale pink.
White Swan — single: white.

---

*Seedling of *saluenensis* x *cuspidata* parentage.
**Seedling of *saluenensis* x *reticulata* parentage.
Both illustrated on page 43.

reticulata seedling

Salutation

alba grandiflora

x Cornish Snow

We are indebted to the Royal Horticultural Society for the above illustrations of camellias which have received the Award of Merit at their flower shows. The award for Salutation was made March 24, 1936, and for the other varieties on February 17, 1948. (Ed.)

"CAMELLIA BLOOM FORMS"

Among the hundreds of varieties available at the present time, gardeners may select camellia blossoms ranging in color from the purest whites through many shades of cream, pink and red.

Not only are there many shades of pink and red, but also different casts or tints including yellow, orange and blue undertones. Blossoms with variegations of these colors ranging from thin stripes to large blotches are also available.

Petals vary in texture from gardenia type to thin poppy like. The petals of some varieties are flat and smooth while others are ruffled and fimbriated.

Some varieties have blooms as small as a silver dollar while others are six or seven inches across. Size alone, however, is not necessarily an indication of the beauty of the bloom.

No small part of camellia's present day popularity is due to the many beautiful shapes or forms of blooms. These range from delicate singles to formal doubles.

In setting up a guide for show committeemen, the American Camellia Society suggests that blooms fall in the following classifications:

Single — (Amabilis)
Semi-Double — (Donckelari)
Incomplete Doubles
    (a) Center petals large (Gloire de Nantes)
    (b) Center petals small (Elegans (Chandler)
    (c) Center petals inter-mixed (Nobilissima)

PEONIFORM
Marchioness of Exeter

SEMI-DOUBLE
Tricolor (Siebold)

44

Complete Doubles
    (a) Regular imbricated (Alba Plena)
    (b) Incomplete imbricated (Mathotiana)
    (c) Tiered (Candidissima)
    (d) Irregular (Prof. C. S. Sargent)

This is an excellent classification and is being used by many show committeemen in conducting shows in cooperation with the American Camellia Society.

Many nurserymen list bloom forms in a somewhat different manner. The following guide from the Oregon Camellia Society year book is fairly representative of these listings:

Single — one row of not over seven petals, with a prominent cluster of stamens in the center of the bloom. Examples, Amabilis — Kimberley.

Semi-double — two or more rows of petals, lying flat, or standing slightly apart, surrounding a cluster of stamens. Examples, Finlandia — Ethrington White.

Anemone — a flower with one or more rows of large outer petals with the center a convex mass composed of stamens and petaloids intermingled. Examples, Elegans (Chandler)—Warratah.

Peoniform — a deep rounded flower with several rows of outer petals, with the center a mass of twisted stamens and petaloids. Examples, Daikagura — Debutante — Kumasaka.

Incomplete double or Rose Form — formal imbricated type flower often showing stamens when fully open. Example, Mathotiana.

Complete Double — formal imbricated type flower showing no stamens. Examples, Alba Plena—C. M. Hovey.

DOUBLE
Mathotiana Variant

SINGLE
Amabilis

MRS. FREEMAN WEISS

The variance in bloom forms of camellias growing on the same bush is shown in this illustration. The top flower has five distinct "crowns" with stamens in each while the lower blossom has a single cluster of stamens in the center.

PACKING AND SHIPPING FLOWERS

It is natural that camellia growers will want to share the beauty of their flowers with their friends. As these friends often live in other sections of the country one of the prevalent questions is how to pack and ship blossoms.

It has been proven that freshly opened blooms will last longer when picked in the cooler morning or evening hours, preferably morning. The bloom should be cut with sharp shears and short stems.

Once cut care should be taken to avoid bruising and the blooms should not be allowed to touch each other.

FASTEN BLOOMS

FASTEN BLOOMS

Flowers that are to be shipped or carried any distance should be secured to avoid jarring and bruising. This may be accomplished by cutting a piece of cardboard the same size as the bottom of the box that is to be used for shipping. The stems of the flowers are then wired or sewed to this piece of cardboard. As a further precaution a piece of cotton batting is placed between the flowers and cardboard.

In fastening the flowers small hairpins may be used when fine wire is not available. Plenty of room should be left between flowers to prevent bruising.

SPRAY BLOSSOMS

Once the blooms are securely fastened the cardboard is placed in the container and is in turn fastened to the bottom of the box by a wire or other means. The flowers should then be sprayed gently but thoroughly with cool water and an additional piece of cotton batting or sheeting placed over them. Flowers cared for  in this manner should last for several days, particularly when kept in a cool condition. The outside container should naturally be strong enough to withstand the hazards of shipping.

LARGEST *RETICULATA?*

The plant of Camellia *reticulata* growing in the University of California Botanical Garden and shown in the photograph is not much over 20 years old. It has repeatedly been topped because it was growing through the top of the lathhouse. Some years ago someone broke into the lathhouse and tore off approximately ⅛ of the plant. Then too, many thousands of scions have been cut from the plant for distribution to nurserymen. Hence, the present size of the plant is probably approximately ½ the size it would have attained under normal conditions of culture.

In 1946 a count of flowers was given up after 487 had been counted and probably in an average year the plant will produce about 500 blooms. If partially disbudded the flower size is somewhat increased. Apparently the majority of the plants of *reticulata* offered during recent years by Pacific Coast nurserymen had their origin in the plant photographed.

The blossom shown on the Frontispiece (page II) is from this plant. Both photographs were furnished by Director T. H. Goodspeed, Professor of Botany and Director of the University of California Botanical Gardens.

Souv. de Bahuaud Litou

Pink Poppy

GIGANTEA

PRINCESS BACIOCCHI

LADY CLARE

TRICOLOR RED

DAITERIN

WINTERING IN COLD CLIMATES

During the past few years, scientific experts have carried on extensive research regarding the propagation and culture of plants under artificial light. Various experimental as well as commercial tests have been made using electric light bulbs and fluorescent lamps as a supplementary means of lighting to bring about early bloom and as the only source of light for both propagating and growing plants.

In hopes that brief information regarding these experiments will enable amateurs who live in cold climates to successfully winter camellias, we have corresponded with many of these authorities and asked:

Can camellias (grown in containers, thereby avoiding root disturbance each time the plant is moved) be successfully stored in basements or other semi-warm locations where natural light is poor or nonexistenet during the winter months when the plants are in a comparatively dormant state?

Some of the answers received are given in the following paragraphs in hopes of both extending the "Camellia Belt" and that amateur growers under experimentation will make new discoveries regarding the benefits of artificial light and dormant storage.

BASEMENT STORAGE WITH ARTIFICIAL LIGHT

To date, no actual tests of storing camellias under artificial light during the winter have come to our attention. A local grower has, however, successfully concluded the following experiment. On March 1, he placed several transplanted rooted camellia cuttings in a dark box and placed a fluorescent light unit containing two forty-watt daylight type tubes approximately one foot above the tips of the plants. At this time neither the ones used in the experiment nor those in his regular greenhouse had started new growth.

During the experiment the lights were on approximately sixteen hours each day. At the end of a three-month period when the plants were planted outside, they had attained from two to three inches of new growth and were healthy and had properly colored foliage. On the average they had shown more new growth than plants that had remained in the greenhouse.

FLUORESCENT LIGHT

Dr. D. T. Stoutemyer, now with the University of California College of Agriculture, Agricultural Experimental Station, Division of Ornamental Horticulture, Los Angeles, states that while he was with the U. S.

Department of Agriculture, Glenn Dale, Md., he and his associate, Albert W. Close, grew gordonias, a very close relative of camellias, for long periods of time under fluorescent lamps.

Dr. Stoutemyer further stated that the idea of wintering tender and semi-hardy plants under artificial light should be most interesting. He further feels that future experiments carried on by amateurs and professional growers will develop much additional knowledge regarding the possibilities of fluorescent lighting.

Dr. Stoutemeyer thinks that further experiments will be required and particularly as to the color of tube most beneficial (fluorescent tubes are manufactured in various colors). Experiments to date indicate that 3500-degree white tubes are inducive to root growth and fast but somewhat soft top growth while Daylight type tubes produce a slower but well hardened growth.

DORMANT STORAGE

Dr. Walter E. Lammerts, Rancho Del Descanso, La Canada, California, advises that he has conducted experiments in which he artificially produced the condition of mild cold weather so as to give camellia seedlings an extra cycle of growth. He placed the potted camellias in a cold storage refrigerator at a temperature of 40° F. They were in complete darkness in the refrigerator for over two months and showed no ill effects and resumed vigorous growth as soon as brought back into the greenhouse.

Dr. Lammerts does not believe that artificial light is necessary providing the camellias are dormant during the period of storage. He does believe that potted camellias can be stored in basements in cold climates if temperatures are not too high; 40° or 50° F. would probably be about right although somewhat lower temperatures would do no harm. Active growth would probably start should the temperature be maintained at higher than 50° F.

BASEMENT GREENHOUSE

Mr. B. Y. Morrison, Principal Horticulturist in charge of Division of Plant Exploration and Introduction at U. S. Department of Agriculture Plant Industry Station, Beltsville, Md., answers as follows:

"The only bit of information I can give you is the experience of a friend of mine, an amateur, who has a small fluorescent lighted propagating case which he used in the winter for growing some cuttings and some seed, all of azaleas. When he wanted to remove his cuttings from the case, it was already mid-winter and he had no greenhouse. What he did was to buy some more fluorescent lights, put them on the ceiling of the same basement room where his case was located, and transfer the rooted cuttings directly underneath these lights. I have seen them myself and certainly the plants have grown. The only thing that I would say is that the growth has been more slender and not completely normal.

"If you want to grow your camellias actively through the winter months, I suspect that you would be able to do it, but I question very much whether or not the plants would not show weaker growth after several winters under these artificial conditions. If you do not care to have your plants in an active growing condition, you might make·some adaptation of the old orange house or the even more primitive pit.

"You recall, perhaps, that the orange house of Europe was an ordinary building, usually of brick or stone, without heat and with windows spaced along the sides. The orange trees were grown in tubs out of doors through the summer and in the orange house, or orangery as it was called, in the winter, where they were kept in practically a dormant condition. The device was particularly used in France and the countries bordering the Mediterranean which did not have completely subtropical climates. It was not useful in the north of Europe.

PIT HOUSE STORAGE

"The pit house in its various forms is rather common in the East. I have such a house in my own personal garden and there is absolutely no heat in it. I can take camellias through our winters here as well as so-called 'Indian-azaleas.' There is no freezing if the plants are kept on the soil floor, but there is freezing on the one bench that I have on the south side of the house when the temperature outside drops to 10°. There is no damage on that bench unless the outside temperature drops below zero."

Mr. C. F. Kinman, Senior Pomologist, at the U. S. Department of Agriculture, Plant Industry Station, Beltsville, Md., replied as follows:

"In regard to storing camellias in a basement in cold climates, this could doubtless be done, provided the plants had been grown in pots, tubs or other containers. I would not expect the method to succeed with plants that had been grown in the open and that would have to be removed for storing. It is possible that the use of fluorescent lamps would be beneficial but we do not have evidence from tests with camellias that prove this."

In conclusion it would seem that the methods of wintering may be classified in two ways: (1) the use of artificial light with the idea of maintaining growth as nearly normal as possible. This in turn involves use of higher temperature—namely placing of plants near the basement furnace. And (2) the maintenance of plants in as nearly dormant condition as possible, i.e., in total darkness at temperatures of 40° F. or even lower.

SEASON OF BLOOM

It is difficult to classify camellias into three distinct blooming seasons, as weather, growing conditions and other factors have a bearing on the blooming time of each variety.

The following list will act as a guide, however, in assisting growers to add varieties to their present collection that will enable them to enjoy a longer blooming period.

With the exception of *reticulata*, the varieties listed are *japonicas*. Most *Sasanquas* bloom several weeks ahead of the early *japonicas*.

EARLY *JAPONICAS*

Alba Plena	Daikagura	High Hat
Apple Blossom	Daikagura Red	Imperator
Arejishi	Debutante	Nobilissima*
Comte de Gomer*	Fimbriata	Professor C. S. Sargent*

MID-SEASON *JAPONICAS*

*—Early to Mid-Season
**—Mid-Season to Late

Adolphe Audusson	Duc d'Orleans	Imura
Adolphe Audusson Var.	Duchess of Sutherland	Jarvis Red
Aitonia	Duke of Wellington	Kimberley
Akebono	Elegans (Chandler)*	K. Sawada
Akebono Var.	Elizabeth Arden	Kumasaka
Alba Superba	Elizabeth Boardman	Kumasaka Var.
Alexander Nowland	Emperor of Russia	Lady Clare
Amabilis	Enrico Bettoni	Lady Hume's Blush
Aspasia	Ethrington White	Lady Mary Cromartie
Augusta Wilson*	Eugene Lizze	Lady Vansittart**
Aunt Jetty	Feasti	Lady Vansittart Red**
Beali Rosea	Finlandia*	Lallarook**
Bella Romana	Flame	Latifolia
Caleb Cope	Francine	Lurie's Favorite
California	Frau Minna Seidel	Madame Haas
Cameo Pink*	Gigantea	Magnoliaeflora
Campbelli	Glen 40**	Magnoliaeflora English
Caprice	Gloire de Nantes	Marchioness of Exeter*
Catherine Cathcart**	Gosho-guruma	Marion Mitchell**
Cheerful	Governor Mouton	Martha Brice
Claudia Lee	Grandiflora Alba **	Mathotiana
Cliveana	Haku-Rakuten	Mathotiana Rosea
Coletti Maculata	Hakutsuru	Mena Ladnier
Countess of Orkney	Herme	Mikenjaku
Donckelari	Hibiscus	Monarch**

MID-SEASON *JAPONICAS* —(Continued)

Monjisu
Monjisu Red
Mrs. Abby Wilder
Mrs. Anne Marie Hovey
Mrs. Charles Cobb
Mrs. Chas. Simons**
Mrs. Freeman Weiss
Otome
Otome Red
Peoniflora**
Pink Ball**

Pink Star**
Pope Pius IX
Princess Baciocchi**
Purity
Reticulata
Rev. John Bennett**
Rev. John G. Drayton**
Sara-Sa
Semi-double Blush
Snowdrift
Sophia

Stardust
Sweeti Vera
Tanner William's Red
Te Deum**
T. K. Variegated
Tricolor Red
Tricolor (Siebold)
Triphosa
Vedrine**
White Empress*
White Giant

LATE *JAPONICAS*

Anne Lindbergh
Bessie McArthur
Black Prince
Candidissima
C. M. Hovey
Dante
Eleanor Hagood
Elena Nobile
Elizabeth

Ella Drayton
Fred Sander
Harlequin
Il Cygno
Jean Keer
Kellingtonia
Mathotiana Alba
Matsukasa
Mrs. K. Sawada

Mrs. Lurman
Sarah Frost
Rosea Superba
Rosita
Somegawa
Souv. de Bahuaud Litou
Victor Emmanuel
Ville de Nantes
Ville de Nantes Red

PEAK JAPONICA BLOOMING SEASON

CAPRICE

FRED SANDER

Blossom illustrated is known as Fimbriata Superba (*a sport of* Fred Sander) *in the Northwest. In this area this variety has larger, more fimbriated blossoms than* Fred Sander.

PROPAGATION OF CAMELLIAS

The propagation of camellias by both commercial and amateur growers is usually confined to three methods. These involve raising from seed, starting new plants by means of cuttings or "slips," and various methods of grafting.

The following paragraphs will explain these three methods in detail. Basically the propagation from seed method leads to new varieties and variations of present varieties. The cutting and grafting methods are primarily used to develop new plants of the same variety as that from which the cuttings or graft scions were taken.

CAMELLIAS FROM SEED

A fascinating hobby is open to the camellia enthusiasts who desire to raise camellias from seed. Many of our present popular varieties were originated by commercial growers after years of research and time had been spent in development of cross-pollinated seeds.

Normally several years elapse from the time of planting until the first bloom appears. Amateurs desiring quicker results may follow the example of many commercial men who graft small scions taken from the seedlings to older root stocks.

Camellias are easy to raise from seed. Only the varieties which produce stamen and pollen will seed themselves or can be cross-pollinated. Double varieties as well as most peony and others without stamens do not produce seed.

CAMELLIA SEED

The stamen varieties often produce self-pollinated seed but the number of seeds per plant is slight in comparison with the number of blooms. The self-pollinated seeds rarely produce outstanding plants.

Seed pods are usually about an inch or more in diameter and consist of a thick outer shell and from three to five seeds. When the outer shell opens the seeds are ripe and may be immediately planted.

Seed germination is usually high when planted at the time they become ripe. However, they may be kept for considerable periods of time if packed in peat moss and placed in a refrigerator.

59

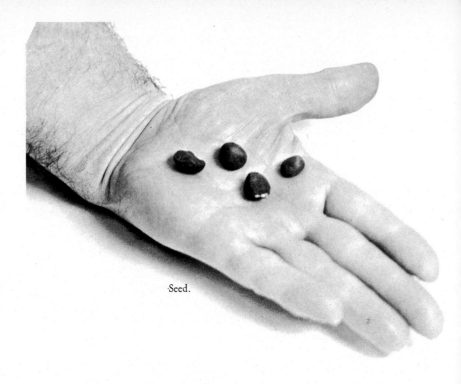

·Seed.

CAMELLIAS FROM SEED

Additional illustrations of new and popular seedlings on pages 62, 64 and 65.

Year-old seedling.

Seedling flower.

A prominent amateur recommends placing seed in a jar filled with damp peat moss kept at room temperature, allowing them to root and then transplanting at a later more convenient time.

Amateur growers wishing to develop choice and new varieties will not be content with self-pollinated seed.

HYBRIDIZING

As with all other seed, hybridizing calls for transferring the pollen from the stamens or anthers of one bloom to the pistils of another. To avoid self-pollenization the stamens are removed from the blossoms that are intended to bear seed. These blossoms are then carefully watched to determine the proper time for pollenization. When such examination shows that the stigma is damp or covered with a sticky or glutinous matter the pollen collected from the stamen of another bloom should be applied by direct contact or with a small fine artist type paint brush. This condition will usually occur during the warmer part of the day.

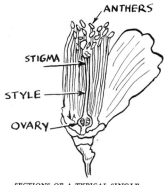

SECTIONS OF A TYPICAL SINGLE
VARIETY CAMELLIA BLOSSOM

Often even hand-pollinated blossoms do not produce seed and several blooms should be pollinated to assure the required seed pod's development.

An experienced hybridizer advises that results are more certain if the "milky" fluid that may be pressed from a broken stamen is applied to the pistil instead of pollen.

Depending upon climatic conditions the pod will usually ripen between September 1 and November 30.

POLLEN MAY BE COLLECTED BY REMOVING
ANTHERS FROM A BLOSSOM.

APPLYING POLLEN TO STIGMA OF EMASCU-
LATED BLOSSOM WITH ARTIST BRUSH.

LADY CLARE ◁

×

◁ GRANDIFLORA
ALBA

=

NEW SEEDLING—MRS. BERTHA A. HARMS

The beautiful new seedling shown at the top of this page is the result of a crossing of Lady Clare and Grandiflora Alba made in 1939 by H. H. Harms. It bloomed for the first time in the spring of 1947 but did not bloom profusely until the 1948 season. The camellia has been named Mrs. Bertha A. Harms in honor of his wife.

Its rose shaped buds have a distinct but pale pink cast. The petals unfurl like those of a rose and open into a pure white semi-double blossom, measuring 5½ to 6 inches across and having 14 wavy crepe-like petals and over 100 yellow stamens. The seedling is a medium-late bloomer with long lasting flowers and an 8 to 10 week blooming season. As the blossoms mature the color changes from a pure white to a soft delicate pink.

The plant is a medium-fast grower featuring an upright open growth and medium size pointed leaves, quite similar to the mother plant's (Lady Clare) foliage.

The theory of many experienced hybridizers that the mother plant influences the hardiness and foliage and the father the bloom form and color, is borne out in this fine camellia.

———— ❋ ————

ANOTHER FINE SEEDLING—JOSEPH PFINGSTL

Was awarded the American Camellia Society Award of Merit on the basis of the judges' decision at the 1948 Montgomery, Alabama, show.

The camellia, developed by Mr. Emmett J. Pfingstl of Montgomery, features large, dark-red, incomplete double blossoms with wavy outer-petals that become fluted and surround a group of yellow stamens. It is a vigorous grower with a long blooming season and long lasting blossoms.

Seed may then be planted in a mixture containing approximately one-half sandy loam and peat moss and one-fourth leaf mould or compost

(or if preferred, some of the new planting medium such as Vermiculite may be substituted). The seed should be covered with approximately one-half inch of the same medium. A light sprinkling of ·aluminum sulphate or sulphur on the soil will help prevent damping-off and produce a desirable acid condition when soil is used. When other medium is used aluminum sulphate will help produce the acid condition that camellias like.

GERMINATED
SEED

Amateurs who own a greenhouse or hot bed with "bottom heat" may expect germination within four to twelve weeks. If a greenhouse is not available seed may be placed outside in a protected place where they will sprout and send down a tap root and be ready to start top growth with the following spring.

When four to six leaves have formed, plants should be potted or transplanted in an outside shaded location. The tip of the tap root should be pinched off at this time to encourage root branching. If this is not done, the tap root will soon advance to a length of 15 to 18 inches and shock of later transplanting will be hard on the young plant. (Note illustration.)

CUT TAP ROOT

Even though careful hand pollenizing methods are followed the chances of producing worthwhile new varieties are small. Should the bloom prove to be of mediocre value the plant may still be used as root stock for grafting purposes.

There is always a chance of the development of some rare new variety, even a new choice yellow, which is the ambition of prominent commercial growers, or new improved fragrant varieties.

MENDEL'S LAW

Camellia enthusiasts who are really serious in their desire to create a new variety and are familiar with Mendel's Law may wish to let their new plant cross-pollinate itself or again be hand pollenized in hopes of attaining their desired goal in the second generation.

MRS. K. SAWADA (Pat. No. 481)   WHITE EMPRESS

ROYAL WHITE   LIBERTY BELL

WHITE KING   FRIZZLE WHITE

Varieties illustrated above and on the following page are popular seedlings developed by
Mr. K. Sawada, Crighton Station, Mobile, Alabama.

ROBERT NORTON   K. SAWADA (Pat. No. 431)

LURIE'S FAVORITE   QUEEN BESSIE

VICTORY WHITE   WHITE GIANT

CAMELLIAS FROM CUTTINGS

A large number of the camellia plants on the market today were propagated by commercial growers by means of cuttings.

Successful propagations of camellias by cuttings involves constant care which the amateur grower is often unable to lend. The professional grower carefully watches such conditions as humidity and bottom temperature at all hours of the day These have an important bearing on the success of this method of propagation.

SEMI-HARD CUTTINGS

Hence in the belief that the amateur grower will find propagation from seed and graft methods more interesting and practical, and as growing by means of cuttings is amply covered in most books pertaining to propagation, only the essential points of this method are mentioned.

Should he desire to start from slips he should take semi-hard cuttings from current growth. The time or season for such cuttings will vary with climatic conditions. Normally the correct time is when new growth has partially turned brown and will snap or break when bent between fingers.

At this period of development the end of the branch containing approximately four leaves should be cut from the parent plant, as shown at right A slanting cut is made with a sharp knife just below the fourth leaf. The third and fourth leaves are then removed about one-eighth of an inch from the stem (illustrated at left) and the stem of the plant inserted in the rooting medium.

2

1

Experiments to date seem to indicate that the application of one of the plant hormones to the ends of cuttings is beneficial in developing stronger root systems sooner.

The rooting medium may consist of a combination of sand and peat moss or Redwood Bark Mulch or Vermiculite. The addition of a slight amount of aluminum sulphate or sulphur is often considered advantageous as it produces a beneficial acid condition.

Many commercial men prefer to use sharp damp sand alone and do not add peat moss.

It is important that cuttings be shaded from direct rays of the sun. This may be accomplished by tacking white cloth to the sash of the cold frame or greenhouse.

GULF GLORY
(GRANDIFLORA ALBA)

DAWN

The *Sasanquas* illustrated are photographic reproductions of water color sketches by Mr. K. Sawada. Naturally the black and white reductions do not do justice to the sketches or the blossoms but are reproduced to show the variance in bloom form of *Sasanquas* which are becoming more popular because of new varieties, early blooming season and hardiness.

Brief descriptions of the varieties illustrated follow: (Each of the varieties was originally imported from Japan, except Gulf Glory which was originated by Mr. Sawada from seed imported from Japan in 1932.)

GULF GLORY (Grandiflora Alba) a self-white, 8 or 9 petals and numerous stamens. Blooms later than most varieties. Medium, upright, spreading growth.

DAWN (Akebona) porcelain white, semi-double, with wavy, crinkled petals, a few petaloids and numerous stamens. Tips of some petals are faint pink. Upright and compact but slow grower, very hardy.

MINE-NO-YUKI (Snow-on-the-Mountain) semi-double to double, self-white with central mass of about 25 small petaloids intermixed with about the same number of stamens. Fast grower with spreading branches.

USU-BENI (Usuiro Kantsubaki) semi-double to double, soft lavender pink with some white variegation. Has petaloids intermixed with stamens. Compact slow grower.

MINE-NO-YUKI

USU BENI

It requires approximately fifty to ninety days for slips to root. After the roots are approximately one to two inches long the plant may be carefully removed from rooting medium and transplanted in a soil mixture consisting of two-thirds sandy loam and one-third peat moss. Many growers add a small amount of commercial fertilizer, providing the medium has been prepared well in advance and allowed to mellow or age.

Great care should be used in transplanting. Amateurs may have greater success by waiting until the next growing season. (The loss in transplanting rooted cuttings is much higher if the work is done when camellias are in a dormant or non-growing cycle.)

ROOTED CUTTING

CAMELLIAS FROM GRAFTS

Propagation by means of grafts offers many advantages for the amateur grower. Accomplishments made possible by graft are "conversion" of common hardy varieties into improved new and interesting camellias; assurance of hardier root stocks for new popular varieties and more rapid propagation of improved types.

Common methods of grafting are stump or cleft, side, veneer and inarching. Although each of the above methods will be explained, the average amateur will probably more often use the stump and side methods.

GENERAL INSTRUCTIONS

Regardless of method the following steps should be followed.

Scions do best when inserted approximately when buds begin to swell, indicating that new growth is starting.

It is important to have the cambium layer, or growing tissue, of the scion in direct contact with the same tissue of the root stock. The cambium is a very thin layer of cells found between the bark and the sapwood that produces new wood and bark cells that carry the plant's foods.

Cambium tissue can not be seen without the aid of a microscope. The cells lie directly under the bark and are the ones that pull apart when bark is peeled. In peeling part of the cells remain on the underside of the bark and part on the wood.

68

Bessie McArthur

DONCKELARI

MONJISU

ALEXANDER NOWLAND

UNCLE SAM

KUMASAKA

After the scion and root stock have been carefully joined, they should be wrapped with grafting bands. (These are rubber bands about ¼ inch wide that hold the scion firmly in place and at the same time will expand to allow for growth.) At least two leaves should be left on scions.

PROTECTION OF GRAFTS

Arrangements must now be made to prevent the cut surfaces from drying out until the union takes place. Professional growers often employ a graft bench or "sweat-box" in their greenhouse when grafting camellias. The amateur may follow their example or when grafting outside may apply damp peat moss to a height slightly above the union and cover the entire plant with some convenient air-tight container such as a jug from which the throat has been removed.

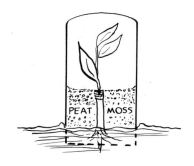

PROTECT GRAFTS

From the start the graft should also be protected from direct rays of the sun. A piece of burlap placed over the jug and weighted at the bottom by soil to prevent blowing will accomplish this.

It is wise to maintain this humid air-tight condition for several weeks after it is assured that the graft has "knit or healed." The "knitting" usually requires six to ten weeks. Then the jug may be gradually withdrawn. Both the scion and union are very tender and should be "seasoned" by lifting the container only a little at a time and should be shaded.

The beginner may prefer the side graft method as the parent or root stock is less apt to be killed should the graft be unsuccessful.

SIDE GRAFT

A side graft is made by cutting the root stock downward and inward slightly above the ground level with a sharp knife. The cut should be of sufficient length to fully receive the wedge shape edge of the scion. The scion then should be slipped into the root stock in such a manner that the cambium tissues join.

If a hardy variety is used as the base the height of the graft may be a determining factor as to the future sturdiness of the plant. In colder climates many growers rec-

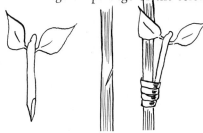

SIDE GRAFTS

Top
Making slanting cut in stock
plant.

Center
Inserting scion.

Lower
Year old side graft on year old
stock.

CLEFT or STUMP GRAFTS

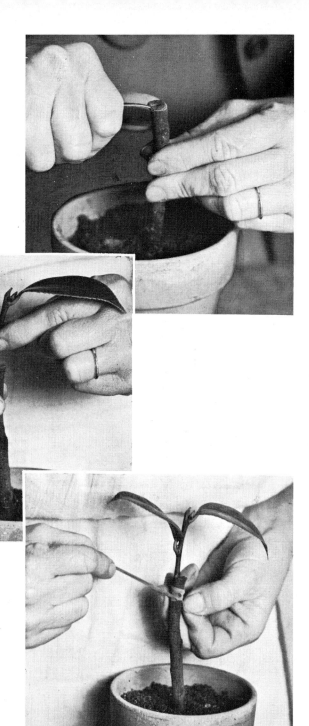

Top
Splitting stock.

Center
Insert scion—align
cambium tissue.

Lower
Binding with rubber
band.

ommend that side grafts be placed several inches above the ground level while in warmer climates they may be inserted closer to the root of the plant.

In general a side graft is quite successful where a small size stock or base plant is involved.

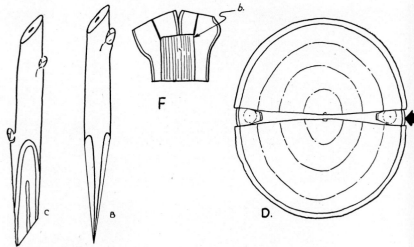

CLEFT GRAFT

A stump or cleft graft is made by cutting straight across the stock (usually that of a larger plant) and then splitting the stump down the middle with a sharp knife or wedge to a sufficient depth to receive the scion or scions.

Success is enhanced by placing a scion at each edge of the split, again being careful that the cambium bark of the scions and root stock join. This offers a double opportunity for the growth of a scion and at the same time tends to relieve pressure caused by the tendency of the root stock, particularly in larger plants, to rejoin.

The scion or scions should be shaped with a knife so they will fit into the split of the stump without undue wedging.

A. Cleft grafting with scion in place.

B. One view of scion showing sloping cut with narrow edge showing.

C. Scion showing broadside view. Two leaves should be left on camellia scions.

D. View from above, showing scions with cambium layers in line. Note that with large stock the scions are indented in order to have the cambiums meet.

F. Diagram of the growth of two scions, one originally at (b). New growth is laid down over the old scions and the old stock, forming a purely mechanical union.

A—One-year graft on three-year
  stock.
B—One-year grafts on six-year
  stock.

C—20 to 24 inch *saluenensis*.
D—10 to 15 inch *japonica*.

VENEER GRAFT

This type differs from the side graft in that the entire outer portion of the root stock is removed as shown in the illustration. The scion is then carefully joined, again seeing that the cambium bark joins at least on one side, depending upon the width of the scion in comparison with the root stock.

INARCH GRAFTS

Inarch grafting calls for a portion of the bark of each plant being removed as shown in the accompanying illustration. The plants are then joined, again being certain that the cambium bark touches, and are carefully bound as in other grafting methods.

As in the case of side or veneer graft, the root or base stock usually remains uninjured in case a successful graft is not accomplished when this method is used.

Later when plants have adhered or united one is cut from its root and allowed to grow on to the other. In other words the new variety desired is cut slightly below the graft or adhesion. At the same time the top is removed above the union from the root stock plant. Providing the graft was made well above the root, as indicated in the drawing, the base or roots of both plants should live.

While this method is fairly simple and successful it offers one main disadvantage in that it is grafted so high above the root structure that the base of the old or common variety is apt to throw out side branches below the union. Remove these.

REMOVAL OF OLD GROWTH

In the case of side and veneer grafts the top growth of the old plant should be cut back within approximately six inches of the graft when a successful union has been completed. Later all growth above the union should be removed.

LAYERING

Layering is another method sometimes used in propagating camellias.

Because of the upright habit of growth it is usually impractical to bend a branch to ground level to be covered with damp soil, peat moss or other rooting medium. This difficulty may be overcome by employing the air or Chinese layering method.

This means of propagation calls for notching the stem of the camellia and then keeping the "opening" surrounded by a damp rooting medium. A ball of sphagnum moss tied around the notch will be all that is necessary providing the moss is kept damp at all times. Some growers prefer to saw a flower pot or other container in two; fit and tie it around the notch; and fill it with a damp rooting medium.

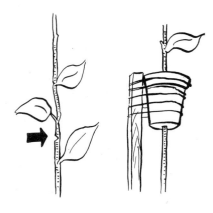

CHINESE LAYER

CAMELLIAS FROM CUTTINGS

A—"Heel" forms   B—First roots
C—Mature roots   Right—Year-old plant

CAMELLIA CORSAGES

The rapid increase in popularity of camellias has been reflected in the floral trade. Reports from all parts of the country, including large eastern markets, advise that camellia corsages are becoming more and more popular. A recent United Press article describing one of the largest weddings in recent times stated, "the bride carried a bouquet of white camellias combined with small white butterfly orchids and lilies of the valley."

The following article on corsages which appeared in the Oregon Camellia Society's year book, "Camellias As A Hobby," explains in detail how the amateur grower may make attractive camellia corsages.

PINK BALL CAMELLIA CORSAGE

Camellia growers who have been content to pin their choicest blossom, unadorned, to their dress or coat lapel will find a new satisfaction when they learn the simple steps required to arrange them into professional-looking corsages. By proper arrangement the leaves will form an attractive background and a firm setting for the blossom to prevent its dropping from the stem.

MATERIALS

Materials needed are wire in sizes 22 or 24, depending on the weight and size of the flower. This may be obtained in 18-inch lengths. When cut in half they usually work better with short-stemmed flowers and leaves. Fine wire may also be bought on spools, and cut to the desired lengths. Green tape and matching or contrasting ribbon complete the materials list.

The blossoms used for the corsage should be freshly cut and recently blossomed flowers. Carefully remove the blossom from its inflexible stem. Then slightly cup the blossom between the fingers of one hand and insert two lengths of wire at right angles directly through the base of the flower. (Illustration 1.)

The wire should be deep enough to anchor the flower. Next bend the four wire ends back around the flower-base to form a new and flexible "stem," twist together (Illustration 2) and wrap spirally with tape.

The camellia leaves are prepared by inserting a loop of wire about a half inch from the base, circling the central vein. (Illustration 3). Twist the ends of the wire firmly around the short stem of the leaf and into a single strand, then tape the new artificial stem.

ARRANGEMENTS

Conventional arrangement is to place three leaves triangularly behind the camellia, winding their wires about the central camellia wires. (Illustration 4.) Ribbon, looped and wired separately, may be added to complete the corsage, or the flower may be worn without ribbon or other trim, particularly for daytime or street wear.

If a more elaborate corsage is desired, continue from the basic arrangement with additional flowers, adding a pair of leaves with each flower to form a spray.

Other arrangements will suggest themselves as practice brings skill in manipulating materials and seasonable garden blossoms. Lilies-of-the-valley, violets, forget-me-nots, or other small blossoms may be added for variety.

VARIETIES

Suitable as single-flower corsages are such varieties as Gosho-guruma, Lady Clare, Finlandia, Kumasaka, or Elegans (Chandler).

Single or semi-double types are easier to use than full doubles, the doubles are not only more difficult to work with, but often have a heavy appearance when worn. Small and medium-sized varieties adapt best to combinations of two or more flowers. Recommended are Amabilis, Claudia Lee, Debutante, Tricolor and the stand-bys of every garden, Purity and Frau Minna Seidel.

CAMELLIA CORSAGES

Top
LADY HUME'S BLUSH

Center
KATHLEEN
(A new pink seedling, popular in the
Northwest.)

Lower
CHEERFUL

CAMELLIAS IN ARRANGEMENTS

Probably no flower lends itself to more beautiful arrangements than the camellia. The various sizes, colors and forms of blooms offer many possibilities of attractive arrangements.

Because of the wide variety of bloom forms, colors, and types, all of the basic elements of flower arrangements such as contrast, harmony, balance, unity, form, line, and color may be advantageously adopted according to the tastes of the individual.

Depending upon individual tastes, camellias may be beautifully arranged in more or less ornate, silver, crystal and china containers or in more simple bowls, including plain and Early American glass and metal containers.

Because of its symmetry and texture the camellia's foliage tends toward artistic arrangements. Many growers hesitate to cut long branches and have found that the foliage of ivy, myrtle and magnolia may be advantageously used instead as they offer similar rich texture.

Camellias are so lovely in themselves that many other flowers do not look well when combined in arrangements. However, in certain sections of the country early flowering tree blossoms such as peach, plum and cherry are in bloom at the same time and blend well. Their long slender and often curved branches add height and line.

CENTER OF INTEREST

In using these combinations it is well that they be of a lighter shade or color than the camellias used, as height adds weight. Camellias may be used at the base for center of interest and may be brought slightly over the edge of the container.

Variety for those who prefer shallow arrangements may be accomplished by placing camellias in plates or shallow bowls. In so doing no other flower need be added.

Camellias may then be grouped, using the larger flowers at one edge and graduating them along the sides with smaller blossoms and buds. This method of arranging is usually most interesting when sufficient space is left between the blooms and one side appears longer or "heavier" than the other. Tip ends of ivy or myrtle or camellia foliage may be used for greenery.

SELECT CORRECT SHADES

The value of shades and tints of the various blooms deserves careful consideration in arrangements. Many camellias are in shades of pink but upon careful examination some of these have a basic blue tint while others may have tints of yellow. These blooms should not be used together for the most effective arrangements. The various red camellias are also shaded from the yellowish or orangish tints to hues of blue or purple.

Reds and pinks may be used together, however, providing both colors have the same basic tints. In using these two colors in combination darker and larger flowers should be placed at the base of the container to form the axis or center of interest for the arrangement.

(The above article appeared in "Camellias As A Hobby" and should assist in making the camellia blooming season the high spot of the year for flower arrangers.—ED.)

CLAUDIA LEE ARRANGEMENT

ASPASIA

SAN FRANCISCO CAMELLIA SHOW

C. M. HOVEY

Arrangement at 1946 show sponsored by San Francisco Camellia Society.

Photo courtesy S. F. News.

CAMELLIA LEAVES

Camellia foliage is a source of year round beauty that even the most inexperienced and casual observer admires and enjoys. To the experienced grower, the individual leaves that make up this evergreen foliage are a source of valuable information. The camellia fancier can often determine both the variety of plant as well as its health and growing conditions by observing the leaves.

The leaves of many varieties are almost as much a means of identification as are its blossoms. They vary in shape, from long narrow ones to almost round leaves and also vary as to texture and color as well as size. Some have almost saw-toothed edges while others have smooth.

LEAVES IDENTIFY VARIETY

The photographs accompanying this article show some of the variances in shape. Illustrated are left to right, Enrico Bettoni, Mikenjaku, Lady Clare and Arejishi. Camellia leaves not only help identify the variety but also indicate the plant's vitality, health and the suitability of growing conditions.

It is natural that camellias as well as all other broad-leaf evergreens shed a certain proportion of their leaves each year, normally in the case of camellias about one-third. Sometimes the profuse blooming, large flowered varieties such as Lady Clare shed considerably more shortly after blooming. Excessive leaf fall should warrant further study as to its cause. Often it would indicate that the plant had used up too much of its stored plant food and vitality during the blooming season; hence, unless investigation shows that disease, too deep planting or pests are causing trouble, an application of fertilizer may be the only requirement.

ENRICO BETTONI   MIKENJAKU   LADY CLARE   AREJISHI

TOO MUCH FERTILIZER

As mentioned in the article on fertilizing, camellias require only enough feeding to maintain a healthy growing condition and development of buds and blossoms. Too much fertilizer is more detrimental to a plant growing under desirable soil conditions than too little. By the leaves, the experienced observing grower can often determine when too much fertilizer has been applied as the outer edges are apt to lose their natural color and start turning yellow as indicated in Sketch 4.

SOIL ACIDITY

Should the area around the veins of the leaves start turning yellow (Illustration 5) and no other cause be apparent, the practical gardener will usually apply an application of some soil acidifier, knowing that the plants have responded to this treatment under similar circumstances in the past.

PESTS

An excessive number of holes in the leaves, either on the edges (Sketch 1) or center (Sketch 2) would indicate that pests are at work. These can usually be fought by giving the foliage a thorough sprinkling with the garden hose. If this treatment does not stop the damage, further study of the camellia as well as surrounding shrubs will probably indicate the type of pest that is doing the damage and what type of commercial spray should be used. If yellow spots appear on leaves a check for sucking insects is advisable.

SUNBURN

Leaves also warn the grower if the camellia has been planted in too sunny a location. In this case, they scald or turn brown as indicated in Sketch 3. Even in climates with cooler summers where most camellias may be planted in full sun, some leaves scald. Plants that show an excessive number of burned leaves should be moved to a partially shaded location. The transplanting should not be done until the proper season, however.

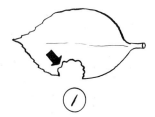

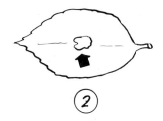

Camellias as well as other shrubs planted in full sun should not be sprinkled during the heat of the day. Drops of water on the leaves act as a magnifying glass and are apt to cause burn.

"BRANDING"

A practical gardener has advised that he uses camellia leaves as a means of temporarily labeling or "branding" plants until a more permanent label can be applied. This is accomplished by lightly printing the name on the soft back side of the leaf with a lead pencil. This causes a slight bruise which turns brown. Pro-viding the writing was not done heavily enough to cause an exces-sive bruise, the lettering can be read from either side of the leaf as long as it remains on the plant. If the lettering is done in the normal left to right hand writing manner as shown in Sketch 7 it will ap-

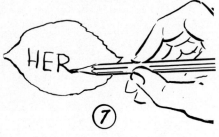

pear in reverse as in Sketch 6 when viewed from the front of the leaf.

A commercial grower advises that he labels plants by punching holes or notches in the leaves according to a pre-arranged code system.

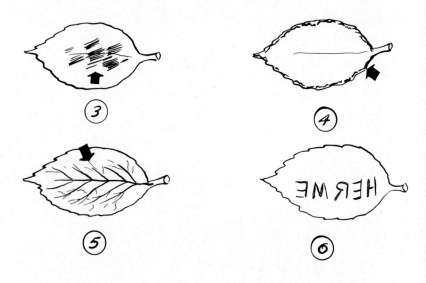

PINK STAR

GOSHO-GURUMA VAR.

ADOLPHE AUDUSSON

VICTOR EMMANUEL

GLEN 40

REV. JOHN G. DRAYTON

PLANT DISEASES AND INSECT PESTS OF CAMELLIAS

A. E. Morrison

The number of species of plants which do not play host to some form of plant or animal life are few indeed. The camellia is not an exception, and while it may, at times, be subjected to serious injury, such conditions are not too common or general. In this respect it may be considered, as a plant, to have even fewer pests than many other garden favorites. A few general precautions, which also apply to other plants, will definitely pay dividends with camellias.

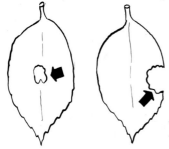

"CAMELLIAS HAVE EVEN FEWER PESTS THAN MANY OTHER GARDEN PLANTS"

Plant diseases and insects develop and assume injurious proportions when conditions favorable to their development are maintained in a garden. Often these conditions may not be too favorable to the host and it suffers through lack of ability to withstand the effects of infestations of either diseases or insects or even both. Generally speaking plant diseases and most insects require protection. This protection may be found in dense growth under crowded conditions from too close plantings of camellias or when they are closely planted among other species of plants. Adverse conditions may also occur in lath or hot houses.

A circulation of air through the plant, some sunshine, good soil drainage permitting frequent waterings of both tops of plants and the soil surface, a soil condition to permit aeration of the roots all aid in developing and maintaining the camellia in a healthy condition and discourages attacks by pests.

Very few pests of camellias are common to all camellia growing centers. This may well be understood when all of the growing conditions of the various sections of the United States are carefully considered. Areas vary from high summer humidity and rains to low summer humidity and only winter rains; and then conditions in between the two extremes. We also find a wide range of soil and water types. Certain of our insects, and definitely the diseases, react to these different conditions and a separate consideration of the handling of pests under each is a desirable method of meeting the problem.

Too often we find a garden enthusiast reading, and then putting into practice, information written and intended to correct conditions com-

CAMELLIA PESTS

Left—Camellia scale (*Lepidosaphes camelliae*) on camellia leaf, slightly enlarged.

Center—Left—Soft brown scale (*Coccus hesperidum*) enlarged about 5 times.

Right—Camellia scale enlarged about 5 times.

Lower—Left—Camphor scale (*Pseudaonidia duplex*) enlarged about 7 times.

Right—Tea scale (*Fiorinia theae*) on camellia leaf enlarged about 9 times.

Photos courtesy of Dept. of Zoology-Entomology, Alabama Agricultural Experiment Station, Auburn, Alabama.

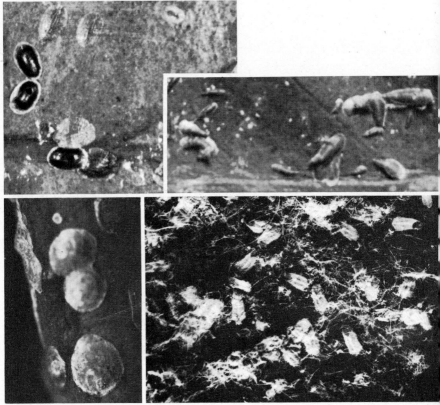

pletely dissimilar to those in his own garden and instead of correcting an imaginary condition he may even go so far as to injure plants through the needless application of materials.

It is not necessary, neither is it desirable, to spray camellias, nor any other plant, unless the need for such treatment is evident. For the purpose of this article mention will be made only of those insects and diseases which may need some attention. Insects not of common occurence or of minor importance are omitted.

SCALE

Scale, of various species, makes up the most common group of insects likely to be found on camellias. They may be looked for on the branches, twigs or on either surface of the leaves, depending upon the species present. Evidence of an infestation of scale may be observed by a peculiar light spotting on the upper surface of the leaf; by an abundance of ants visiting the plant; by noticing their presence when encrusted on the foliage or along the twigs. The light spotting of the foliage peculiar to scale damage is due to the sucking action of the insect in removing juices or food from the leaf which interferes with the chlorophyll or green coloring matter. The ants are attracted to the sweet honey dew secreted by some scales. Fungus is often found growing in smears of honey dew giving parts of the plant a dirty, sooty appearance.

Control measures need be applied only where large numbers of scale are easily found on the plant. The application of a spray will not, ordinarily, eliminate all the insects and a few survive even the best spray job. This point should be considered when only a light infestation is noticed on a plant or where a few scale are to be found after a minute examination Natural enemies or climatic conditions may be doing as good a control job, in such cases, as if a spray were applied.

Some of the more important scale insects found on camellias are: three camellia scales (*Parlatoria camelliae*, *Lepidosaphes camelliae*, and *Pulvinaria floccifera*); the Tea, Greedy, Ivy, Chaff and Florida red scales. Many others could be named but they are not important except possibly in some local instances.

The Camellia scale (*Lepidosaphes camelliae*), tea scale (*Fiorinia thea*) and the Florida Red scale (*Chrysemphalus ficus*) are the most important scale insects in the Gulf and Southern States. A second camellia scale, which might be called camellia parlatoria (*Parlatoria camelliae*), Greedy scale (*Hemiberlisia rapax*) and Ivy scale (*Aspidiotus hederae*) are prevalent in some western areas. The camellia scale (*Pulvinaria floccifera*), is usually found on plants in hot house cultivation or in lath houses. It is an interesting scale with a long white egg sack protruding behind the scale body.

95

CONTROL OF SCALE

In using control measures the timing of the spray application is even more important than the material used. The overwintering period is spent by the scale under the protection of a hard shell which completely covers the insects, in the case of armored scales, or by a hardened coating, in the case of the soft or unarmored species. This shell or covering, as the case may be, provides protection from sprays unless a strong penetrating material is used under high pressure. Dormant sprays satisfactory for killing the scale at this period are usually injurious to evergreen foliage and are not practicable to use on camellias.

Some species of scale produce eggs beneath their shell which hatch into "crawlers" (minute insects fully equipped with legs), while others produce living young, also called crawlers. These very small insects, hardly larger than pin points, move about without protection and are very easily destroyed even with a good force of water. Left alone they attach themselves to a desirable place on the plant, insert their beak into the bark or leaf, secrete a waxy covering, lose their legs and power of movement and complete their life cycle. The vulnerable or unprotected period lasts but a few weeks and successful control must be attempted during this time.

Any good oil emulsion spray suitable for foliage use in the summer, at a 1% to 2% strength thoroughly applied under pressure to all parts of the plant above ground will give good control. Avoid use of any oil spray during days of high temperatures or during periods of drying winds.

The maximum hatch of most species of scale insects, on the West Coast, occurs during late May or early June. Spraying should not be delayed beyond mid-July. Recommendations given for the Gulf Coast and Southern States is to spray as soon as danger of frost is over in the spring and a second application being made six weeks later where heavy infestations occur. A follow up spray in September or early October may be necessary in exceptional cases.

Aphids, at least two species, may be found on new tender growth. Their presence, if not detected early, causes a curling of the leaves which gives the insects protection. Ants are attracted to aphids and not only offer them protection from parasites but have been known to move some to other desirable locations. Again the hose may be brought into play as a strong force of water will wash aphids off the plants. A spray containing pyrethrum and oil or pyrethrum and rotenone and oil gives excellent control before the leaves curl. Commercial materials containing these ingredients are offered for sale and carry directions for mixing. Infestations of this pest do not always cover an entire plant and if one does not care to take the trouble of using a sprayer, just take a tablespoon of the mixture and add it to two quarts of water then dip an infested twig into the mixture, give a shake or two and then move on to another infested branch.

Both red spiders and thrips, may at times, and under certain favorable conditions, become a nuisance on camellias, particularly when grown under lath house, hot house or similar growing conditions. Here again the gardener with plenty of good soft water need not use anything else, but where you must use harsher methods the same material suggested for aphids will give these bugs a bad time. Under dry growing conditions a repeat may be in order. Red spiders and thrips are rather difficult to readily see without the aid of a hand lens. When spiders large enough to be easily seen are noticed on camellias forget them because regardless of color they are not red spiders. Red spider is a name applied to a particular group of very small spiders usually considered as mites and they are not always red. The species infesting camellias does not spin a web.

The presence of red spiders and thrips is indicated by a peculiar light spotting which may be observed on the upper surface of the infested leaves. Although they actually feed mainly on the under surface of the leaf the loss of coloring shows on the upper surface.

Three other mites may be found on camellias if one has the patience and ability to make good use of a hand lens of at least 20 diameters. These are the orange camellia rust mite, the purple camellia rust mite and the camellia bud mite. The rust mites are found on the underside of the foliage and when they occur in large numbers cause a peculiar light rusty appearance on the upper surface of the leaves. The orange rust mite has been reported from both the West and Gulf Coast camellia belts. Control measures are rarely needed but the oil-pyrethrum summer spray should work. The camellia bud mite works at the base of the inner surface of the sepals, or bud scales, and is rarely found inside the petals. In the winter they occur inside leaf buds. So far no damage has been attributed to this mite.

LEAF FEEDERS

Various leaf feeders occasionally visit camellias. Evidence of the fact they have been present are holes of various sizes and shapes depending on whether they were caused by flea beetles or grasshoppers. Usually the culprit is foraging on some other garden plant before one is aware of the visit, so why worry about a hole or so in an occasional leaf? Most of the leaf-feeding insects on camellias are night feeders and are rarely seen at work during the day. It is advisable to watch the unfolding leaves in the early spring, that is if you expect every leaf to be perfect. This is a precaution to take in guarding against the work of either the celery leaf tier or the fruit tree leaf roller. The latter insect may be expected where camellias are grown in close proximity to oak trees. These two insects take a slender leaf, perhaps two, carefully fold it about their pale green little worm bodies, sew the edges together with silk thread and in this happy home proceed to eat out the walls of their castle usually working on the edges of the leaf. They emerge into moths and leave behind at least two badly deformed leaves. The folded leaves protect them from spray so for control just unroll the leaf, pick up the little worm and dispose of it any way that suits.

One danger sign to watch for, particularly where camellias are growing in containers, are numerous irregular holes eaten in from the edge of the leaf. They give the appearance of small semicircle bits having been removed from the edge of the leaf. This is typical work of either the Fullers rose weevil or the black vine weevil (let us hope it is the former). Both are night feeders. The work on the foliage is only part of the story and is not serious. The real damage comes from the larvae of the black vine weevil (*Brachyrhinus sulcatus*) which may girdle the trunk of small plants just below the surface of the ground. This incidentally causes the plant to wilt and another good camellia has been lost. The adults are fond of poison baits particularly the type made up of dried apple pulp. This bait is commercially prepared on the west coast for use against the strawberry weevil and is readily available. Dusting the plants with calcium arsenate immediately when new feeding is observed in the spring also discourages further depredations of this insect. Calcium arsenate and cryolite dusts or a spray of lead arsenate can be used and will also check the work of canker worms, caterpillars and other leaf feeding visitors. If the residue appears unsightly it can be washed off after attacks of the insects ends.

DDT has controlled these insects but it is not recommended now as some DDT mixes have been reported damaging camellias in Southern California and until the exact cause of the damage is known this material should not be used on this plant.

Camellias are generally considered resistant to the root knot nematode although some damage has been reported from California. As a precaution the use of soil known to be infested should be avoided.

Earthworms, particularly the species known as night walkers or crawlers, may, on occasion, injure camellias grown in containers by multiplying to the point where the soil is disturbed and loosened around the roots. A small cardboard collar placed around the crown of the plant and forced down firm against the top soil of the container for a few days will cause the worms to cluster immediately below the collar at the surface of the soil. Have a can and fish pole ready, remove the collar and go to work. An old-time remedy for controlling worms in camellia containers is through the use of lime water made by soaking two quarts of lime in about fifty gallons of water overnight. Do not mix or stir up the lime but allow it to settle to the bottom of the barrel and draw off the water from the top using it to soak the soil around the plant. The worms not killed outright will come to the surface and try to escape from the container. The careful placing of drain holes and keeping these holes from being in contact with the ground will prevent worms from entering the containers.

PLANT CONDITION OR DISEASE

The line of demarkation between condition and plant disease is often too fine for the ordinary gardener to appreciate. Plants may be set back or severely injured by improper planting, watering, fertilizing, etc. Smothering of roots by too deep planting or poor drainage may permit otherwise harmless fungi, such as *Phytophthora*, to gain entrance through root lenticels and take over a weakened plant, first evidence of which is a wilting of foliage. The control is prevention by not planting deeper than when received in the container or ball from the nursery; by allowing for settling after planting and by not annually heaping heavy applications of humus over the ground around the plants; by giving the plant sufficient water to keep the ground moist but not saturated; and providing for good drainage in water-retentive soils.

DIE BACK

Die back, or twig blight, sometimes called *Phomopsis*, prevalent in the Gulf Coast area and reported as occurring in Southern California, causes a dying back of twigs, or branches, and even larger limbs on occasion may dry up. At least three species of fungus have been taken from infected material and the specific organism which may be the primary cause of the injury has not been definitely decided upon. Control suggested is the removal of infected twigs or branches, being certain to cut back well beyond the dead area. Even though a fungus is responsible, the disinfecting of cutting tools is a good precaution. A spray containing copper, such as Bordeaux mixture 5-5-5 strength, applied in early spring about the time of the start of new growth is a practice followed in the areas where this die back is common. Flordo spray has also been suggested. The presence of an occasional dead twig in a camellia plant does not necessarily mean *Phomopsis* is present.

A disease of camellia flowers, known as Camellia blossom rot (*Sclerotinia camelliae*) has been prevalent in some sections of the West Coast for several years. This disease occurs in the late winter during wet weather and is evidenced by wet brown discolorations on the petals of the flowers. It may occur on partially opened buds as well as flowers in full bloom. The start of the disease cycle is the appearance of a small brown toadstool ¼ to ¾ inches in diameter with an upturned cap. Spores are shot into the air in a faint smoke-like cloud and with proper moisture in the blossom start their destructive mission. Infected blossoms drop to the ground where a hard dark

BLOSSOM ROT OR SPOT DISEASE

brown or black body of concentrated mycelum forms. This is called a sclerotium which remains dormant until awakened by proper soil moisture and climatic conditions the next year. The disease has not been known to spread from blossom to blossom but must pass through the sclerotium stage. It is primarily a disease of the flowers and causes little or no damage to the plant itself. The most serious consequence of the disease is to growers who grow camellias for the flower market.

CONTROL

Sanitation, that is picking off affected blooms and all blossoms that drop to the ground has been a recommended method of control. A spray of Fermate, one pound dissolved in 100 gallons of water, applied to the

PICK BLOSSOMS

ground around the plants thoroughly wetting the surface of the soil has been found effective for approximately 14 days. It is necessary to make frequent applications during the blossoming period if rains occur. Fermate settles rapidly and the mixture must be constantly agitated in the spray tank. Since the disease may be carried only in the soil around the plants the removal of ½ to ¾ inch of the soil surface of potted plants will prevent carrying the disease into areas in which it is not known to occur.

The disease Oak Root Fungus, so destructive of many plants, will also attack camellias. Ground known to be infested should be avoided in planting. This disease is not carried by oak leaves as has been feared by some gardeners who have avoided the use of oak leaves as a ground mulch.

P.S.—Having concluded this article I drove past a number of old specimen camellias. Some of them are almost a century old. They are still admired for their beauty of form, healthy appearance and the abundance of flowers produced and yet they are growing without any care and little attention. They are not sprayed nor are they fertilized but are living a regal life on their own and may be expected to outlive many of the pampered house plants that we call "our camellias."

———※———

We are indeed indebted to Mr. A. E. Morrison for the above article. Mr. Morrison is Pacific Coast Vice President of the American Camellia Society and Commissioner of State Quarantine Guardian at Sacramento, California. He has studied camellia culture and disease in many sections of the country.

As strawberry root weevil referred to by Mr. Morrison is quite prevalent in the Pacific Northwest we include the following article by Carl Maskey, Garden Advisor for the Oregon Journal.—*Editor's Note.*

———※———

Most plant life is a host to some disease or pest. Camellias are no exception, but the list of pests or diseases causing damage is a small one in the Northwest. Furthermore in the normal process of controlling pest and disease among other vegetation in the average Northwest garden the ones bothering camellias are also taken care of. Very few require special attention or methods of control.

Of the insects attacking camellias here, the so-called strawberry root weevil or *Brachyrthinus ovatus*, a brownish-colored beetle about one quarter inch long with a long snout, is the worst in this area.

These are difficult to control in the larval stage when they feed underground on the roots and cambium layer. The larva is a creamish-colored grub with a brown head. After feeding on the roots and cambium layers of host plants all winter and spring they pupate for a short time and start emerging about the end of May. They do not all emerge at the same time, an important point to bear in mind in control. Shortly after emerging they begin feeding on the leaves of host plants among which are camellias. They feed mostly at night and on dark days.

STRAWBERRY ROOT WEEVIL
Top—Beetle; lower (left)
Grub; right, Pupa.

Spraying the foliage up to three feet with arsenate of lead solution, four teaspoons to one gallon of water, will effectively rid the area of any adult weevil feeding on foliage.

Poison apple based baits are used extensively in control. The bait is spread under host plants. After breeding and reaching maturity, egg laying at the plant's base begins.

When the eggs hatch the larvae begin feeding during the winter and spring. About seven months elapse between larva and adult stage. Usually only young or potted camellias are attacked by weevils.

BUD SHEDDING

Excessive bud shedding on the part of some camellias is more often caused by unfavorable growing conditions than by disease. The beautiful flowers that annually appear on camellias require many months of development. For this reason it is important that the plants be well nourished and watered at all times. Cutting off this supply of food or moisture even for a short period of time, including dry fall months when buds are large and many gardeners have put away their garden hose, may retard growth, keep buds from developing fully and cause them to drop later in the season.

Camellias that are planted too deep or in soil that is heavy or has poor drainage are also susceptible to bud drop. These conditions have a tendency to starve the plants as they are fibrous rooted, surface feeding shrubs. Under such handicaps, camellias are hardly able to receive enough nourishment to sustain themselves and cannot develop bloom.

Sudden cold spells, particularly those followed by warm sun and rapid thawing, are another cause of bud shedding. This is particularly true when early warm spells have caused the buds to swell prematurely.

Many varieties set more buds than even the healthiest plants are able to nourish to maturity. Failure to disbud or remove some of these retards the growth of all buds, resulting in excessive shedding and undeveloped bloom.

Application of an excessive amount of quick acting fertilizer is another cause of bud drop and plant injury. When this is done more nourishment flows through the plant than can be assimilated.

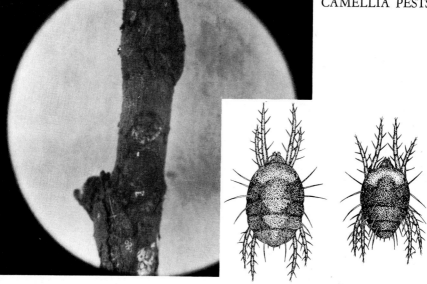

Top—Left—Soft brown scale (*Coccus hesperidum*) on twig enlarged about 7 times.
Right—Red Mite (*Paratetrany chusilicis*) drawing.

Lower—Left—Peony scale (*Pseudaonidia paeoniae*) on twig. Shield removed from scale at center. Enlarged about 7 times.

Lower—Strawberry root weevil (*Brachyrthinus ovatus*) in larva stage. Note bark is eaten from the lower trunk of small camellia bush. This kills plant.

Illustrations courtesy of Department of Zoology-Entomology, Alabama Agricultural Experiment Station except Strawberry root weevil photo by J. G. Bacher, Portland, Ore.

LARGEST CAMELLIA?

Some idea of the size camellias may attain is indicated in the lower illustration of two plants owned by Mrs. Frank Edingers of Hood, Sacramento County, California.

The one in the foreground is a Tricolor (Siebold) that was planted in 1874, is 22 feet tall and has a branch spread of 29 feet and a trunk circumference of 40½ inches. The taller specimen to the rear right is a Purity planted about 1880. A measurement made in December, 1946, showed a height of 28 feet 8 inches.

(Are the camellias illustrated above the largest in America today? We would appreciate hearing from anyone owning or knowing of larger ones.

What might have been a larger camellia was, unfortunately, destroyed by fire. This was a Cheerful and was located in McComb, Mississippi. Mrs. Kenneth G. Price, of McComb, advised that it was 23 feet tall and measured 15 inches in trunk diameter at 15 inches above the ground level when she measured it in the winter of 1942.

The illustration used was supplied by A. E. Morrison. Mr. Morrison also sent the illustration of the oldest camellia, of record, in California. It is a Warratah planted in 1860 by Mrs. Sol Runyon on her ranch about 25 miles from Sacramento and is now owned by Paul Amick shown standing by camellia tree in the top illustration.—*Editor's Note*.)

History of the

American Camellia Society

R. J. Wilmot

At the start of 1940 there were several groups organized throughout the country as camellia clubs or societies and they all were interested in an effort to straighten out camellia nomenclature. No concerted effort was being made, however, to coordinate their work.

At the time of the Camellia Show at Savannah, Judge Arthur W. Solomon entertained a number of growers at a dinner at the General Oglethorpe Hotel, February 10, 1945. After the dinner he called on Dr. H. H. Hume to sum up the situation and after some discussion, a committee composed of D. C. Strother, Chairman, Roy A. Bowden, J. P. Illges, J. G. Gailie, W. T. Wood, G. G. Gerbing, T. J. Smith and R. J. Wilmot was appointed to work out plans for some sort of an organization with the object of standardizing nomenclature.

After much discussion the committee decided the way to clarify the situation was to organize a society, national in scope, to cover all phases of interest. A tentative Charter and By-Laws was drawn up and a call issued for a meeting to be held at the Dempsey Hotel, Macon, Ga., on September 29, 1945. Invitations were sent to 111 and about 50 representing six states were present.

Mr. Strother took the Chair and called on Dr. H. H. Hume and others to discuss the problems. The Charter and By-Laws was presented and adopted with certain changes. A Nominating Committee was appointed by the Chair and the following officers were elected to hold office until the Annual Meeting of 1947:

Dr. H. Harold Hume, President; A. W. Solomon, Vice-President for the Atlantic Coast; Ira S. Nelson, Vice-President for the Gulf Coast; A. E. Morrison, Vice-President for the Pacific Coast; R. J. Wilmot, Secretary; T. J. Smith, Treasurer; A. W. Solomon, A. E. Morrison, D. C. Strother, S. J. Katz, J. P. Illges, R. E. Lee, Directors at Large; State Directors: H. W. Lee, Alabama; Dr. David McLean, California; Mrs. J. H. Churchwell, Florida; J. H. Porter, Georgia; Dr. King Rand, Louisiana; Kenneth G. Price, Mississippi; James Ferger, North Carolina; Paul E. Doty, Oregon; Mrs. Sheffield Phelps, South Carolina; R. A. Merritt, Texas; Miss Marry Bell Glennan, Virginia.

The Secretary was instructed to take necessary steps to incorporate the Society as a non-profit organization under the Laws of Florida.

Following the meeting the sum of $2000.00 was pledged for Patron and Life memberships.

On October 24, 1945, the Charter was submitted to Circuit Judge John A. H. Murphree, Gainesville, Florida, and the Society was incorporated as a non-profit corporation.

Since a name was not available at the Macon meeting for a Washington Director, the membership of that state was circularized in April 1946 and W. L. Fulmer was elected to serve the rest of the year.

On March 29, 1946 the assets and membership list of the Camellia Society of America were turned over by H. T. Conner, Secretary, Macon, Ga. and that Society officially merged with the American Camellia Society.

By January 1, 1947 the membership had grown to 1749 and by July to 2180.

(Membership in the American Camellia Society is open to both amateur and commercial camellia growers. The annual dues of $3.00 and $10.00, respectively, entitle the member to all benefits including receiving a copy of the attractive and instructive Year Book and the mimeographed quarterly.

There are also sustaining, life and patron memberships available. Readers wishing additional information or desiring to join the association should correspond with Mr. R. J. Wilmot, Secretary, American Camellia Society, Gainesville, Florida.—*Editor's Note.*)

OREGON CAMELLIA SOCIETY

The following history and list of activities carried on by the Oregon Camellia Society is included in the hopes that it will acquaint readers who do not belong to an organized club with the advantages and pleasure they may receive from joining the camellia organization in their respective communities.

It is also hoped that the camellia growers living in cities or communities that do not now have a club may see the advantages of organizing one.

(Editor's Note.)

Due to the increasing popularity and interest in camellias in Portland, Oregon and the Northwest a group of camellia enthusiasts met in December, 1941, to discuss the possibility of forming a club. This meeting led to the organization of the Oregon Camellia Society.

The new group again met in January, 1942, drew up by-laws, decided on future meetings and elected Ralph Tetters as first president. The organization has grown from a charter membership of 50 to its present size of approximately 300 members. Most of these members live in and around Portland but many reside in distant states.

Other presidents include H. H. Harms, who served three terms, Joe M. Johnson, Clyde P. Bradley and Robert F. Hamilton, the present president. Since its founding regular monthly meetings are held from September through May. In addition to a short business session these meetings feature informative talks on camellias and camellia culture, slide presentations, a question and answer session and other features.

In recent years the May meeting has been devoted to a plant auction.

A picnic is held each July in place of the monthly meeting. This is always well attended in spite of coming during a season when many members are vacationing at the mountains or beaches.

The first camellia show held in Portland was sponsored by the club in March, 1942, and drew an estimated attendance of 7,000. Annual shows have been held the early part of April each year since with attendance climbing to 20,000.

Hundreds of blooms as well as specimen plants are shown. Other interesting features of the show are displays of corsages and table arrangements. An educational display is also included, where members show cuttings, grafts, and so forth in their various stages of development, and give talks on propagating and growing camellias as well as instructions on making corsages.

Since 1943 the members have annually voted for their favorite camellia, the winner being termed the "camellia of the year." These winners have been: Kumasaka, Lady Clare, Mathotiana, Mikenjaku, Magnoliaeflora, Grandiflora Alba.

During the spring of 1947 a camellia planting was started on the spacious grounds of the Shriners' Hospital for Crippled Children. Specimen plants of each of the "camellia plants of the year" were donated by members and planted at this well attended event. Future "camellias of the year" will be planted each spring. (See illustration, page 39.)

The Society now publishes an annual year book, "Camellias As a Hobby."* This interesting booklet is filled with information on growing, propagating, arranging, etc., as practiced in the Northwest and features a natural color illustration on the cover and back. In addition it lists and describes popular varieties and carries a roster of officers and members of the Society.

The Society is a non-profit organization with an initiation fee of $5 and annual dues of $1.00 per year. Its slogan is "Know, Grow and Show . . ." Camellias As A Hobby.

* While quantities last, copies of this year book may be obtained by sending 30 cents in coin or postage to R. F. Hamilton, President, Oregon Camellia Society, 3444 N.E. 36th Ave., Portland 13, Oregon.

CAMELLIA CLUBS

Camellia clubs or Garden clubs, specializing in camellia culture, are organized in the following cities and communities. The list is probably incomplete but does include all that have come to our attention.

ALABAMA
Bay Minette; Brewton; Daphne; Dothan; Fairhope; Greenville; Mobile.

CALIFORNIA
Berkeley; Fresno County; Glendale; Hollywood; Los Angeles; Pomona; Pasadena; Sacramento; Santa Clara; San Diego; San Francisco; San Jose; San Rafael; Yuba City.

FLORIDA
Crescent City; Gainesville; Hawthorne; Jacksonville; Lakeland; Ocala; Orlando; Palatka; Pensacola; San Mateo; Tallahassee.

GEORGIA
Albany; Atlanta; Augusta; Columbus; Cordele; Ft. Gaines; Gyton; Macon; Marshallville; Middle Georgia; Montezuma; Quitman; Savannah; Thomasville.

LOUISIANA
Alexandria; Baton Rouge; Lafayette; New Iberia; New Orleans; Pineville; Plaquemine; Thibodaux.

MASSACHUSETTS
Boston

MISSISSIPPI
Bay St. Louis; Greenwood; Gulfport; Hattiesburg; Laurel; McComb; Natchez; Ocean Springs.

NORTH CAROLINA
Fayetteville; Raleigh; Rockingham; Wilmington.

OREGON
Coos Bay; Eugene; Salem; Portland.

SOUTH CAROLINA
Charleston; Columbia; Fort Motte; Georgetown; North Charleston; Sumter.

TEXAS
Austin; Houston; Tyler.

VIRGINIA
Norfolk.

WASHINGTON
Seattle.

MONARCH

FINLANDIA VAR.

HAKUTSURU

STARDUST

DUCHESS
DE CASES

CAMELLIA SHOWS

Camellia shows are held annually in the following cities according to advice received from Garden Editors and Garden club members*.

ALABAMA—January or February
Brewton; Dothan; Fairhope; Greenville; Mobile.

CALIFORNIA—February or March
Berkeley; Glendale; Los Angeles; Pasadena; Sacramento; San Francisco; San Jose; San Rafael; Yuba City.

FLORIDA—January or February
Gainesville; Jacksonville; Lakeland; Ocala; Orlando; Pensacola; Tallahassee.

GEORGIA—January or February
Albany; Atlanta; Augusta; Columbus; Cordele; Ft. Gaines; Gyton; Macon; Marshallville; Middle Georgia; Quitman, Savannah; Thomasville.

LOUISIANA—January or February
Baton Rouge; Lafayette; New Iberia; New Orleans; Plaquemine; Thibodaux.

MASSACHUSETTS—January
Boston.

MISSISSIPPI—February or March
Bay St. Louis; Greenwood; Gulfport; Hattiesburg; Laurel; McComb; Natchez; Ocean Springs.

NORTH CAROLINA—January or February
Fayetteville; Wilmington.

OREGON—March or April
Eugene; Portland; Salem.

SOUTH CAROLINA—February or March
Charleston; Columbia; Georgetown; Sumter.

TEXAS—January or February
Austin; Houston.

VIRGINIA—March
Norfolk.

WASHINGTON—March or April
Seattle.

*We will appreciate being advised of any Camellia clubs or shows not included in our lists.

CALIFORNIA CAMELLIA SHOWS

Top—Educational exhibits, one of the features of the 1948 Southern California Camellia Society show held in Pasadena.

Lower—A table setting with camellia arrangements was included in the 1948 Northern California Society show at Oakland. Photo courtesy of John Breuner Furniture Co.

"If Winter Comes"—was the title of the shadow box arrangement which was voted best in show and given the double gold award at the 1948 Norfolk, Virginia, Camellia show.

"Early American Period Flower Arrangement"—took first prize at 1948 Savannah, Georgia, Camellia show, sponsored by the Men's Garden Club assisted by The Garden Council.

Top

SEATTLE CAMELLIA SHOW

Rock garden scene by Clarence Prentice and son, Raymond, at Seattle, Washington, show sponsored by Amateur Gardener's Club.

Lower—Corsage table at Oregon Camellia Society show.

Top—Educational tables at Oregon Camellia Society show.

Lower—"Chinese Garden Scene", the feature exhibit at the 1948 Oregon Camellia Society
show. This beautiful garden was designed by Clarence Prentice and son, Raymond,
Seattle, Washington, landscape architects and creative designers. Both Mr. Prentice and
his son have won national recognition and many awards for their garden show exhibits.

FLORIDA CAMELLIAS

Top

Shadow Box arrangements Jacksonville show.

Center

VICTOR EMMANUEL

A prize winning bloom at Pensacola show.

Lower

GOVERNOR MOUTON

Blossoms being picked by Roland E. Lee, founding president of Escambia County Men's Camellia Club.

"FNPS" photos.

POPULAR VARIETIES

Feeling that camellia hobbyists would like to know what varieties are proving most popular and as a guide in determining which should be included in "Camellias Illustrated" two representative polls have been made.

1. The commercial camellia men who assisted in furnishing facts and data regarding camellia culture in their respective areas and whose firms are listed on pages 147 and 148 were asked to list according to color—

THE BEST SELLING VARIETIES

Varieties are listed in order of the number of mentions received.

RED	PINK	WHITE	VARIEGATED
C. M. Hovey	Frau Minna Seidel	Alba Plena	Herme
Mathotiana	Debutante	Purity	Daikagura
Prof. C. S. Sargent	Pink Ball	Mathotiana Alba	Gigantea
Arejishi	Kumasaka	Finlandia	Donckelari
Cheerful	Francine	Fimbriata	Latifolia
Glen 40	Lady Clare	K. Sawada	Somegawa
Mrs. Chas. Cobb	Magnoliaeflora	Grandiflora Alba	Peoniflora

The same poll indicated that the following varieties increased in popularity during the blooming season when their flowers might be seen.
Red — Arejishi and Victor Emmanuel;
Pink — Debutante, Francine and Magnoliaeflora;
White — Finlandia, K. Sawada and Grandiflora Alba;
Variegated — Lady Vansittart, Alexander Nowland and Donckelari.

☆ ☆ ☆ ☆ ☆ ☆ ☆ ☆

2. Ballots were handed to approximately 2000 of the visitors at the Oregon Camellia Society Show and the vote resulted in the following:

CAMELLIA SHOW SPECTATORS' VOTE

RED	PINK	WHITE	VARIEGATED
Fred Sander	Magnoliaeflora	Grandiflora Alba	Herme
Elena Nobile	Kumasaka	Purity	Tricolor (Siebold)
Flame	Lady Clare	Fimbriata	Elegans (Chandler)
Te Deum	Lallarook	Alba Plena	Daikagura
Emperor of Russia	Pink Star	Caprice	Donckelari
Black Prince	Francine	Amabilis	Adolphe Audusson Var.

Pink was shown to be the most popular color followed by white, red and variegated.

Both polls indicated that women prefer pink varieties and men favor the reds.

CAMELLIAS LISTED ACCORDING TO COLOR

Due to the wide range of shades from the palest pink to the deepest red, it is difficult to list camellias in distinct color classifications.

Then too, climatic and soil condition may affect the color as well as the inclination of camellias to "sport."

"SPORTS"

The tendency of camellias to sport often causes variations in color as well as bloom form. Frequently the blossoms on one branch will be of one color and those on an adjacent branch entirely different. It is not uncommon for pink, red and variegated blossoms to appear on a plant at the same time.

This sporting makes the raising of camellias a series of pleasant surprises. It is due to mutation of the plant cells and the tendency of hybridized plants to revert. Many of the beautiful varieties in gardens today are sports of some other variety. These were propagated by taking cuttings or graft scions from sport branches of the parent plant.

RED

Adolphe Audusson	Flame	Mrs. Charles Cobb
Arejishi	Fred Sander	Otome Red
Aunt Jetty	Glen 40	Pope Pius IX
Black Prince	Gloire de Nantes	Professor C. S. Sargent
California	Gosho-guruma	Sarah Frost
Campbelli	Imperator	Tanner William's Red
Cheerful	Jarvis Red	Te Deum
C. M. Hovey	Kimberley	Tricolor Red
Daikagura Red	Lady Vansittart Red	Vedrine
Elena Nobile	Marion Mitchell	Victor Emmanuel
Ella Drayton	Mathotiana	Ville de Nantes Red
Emperor	Mena Ladnier	Warratah
Emperor of Russia	Monjisu Red	

WHITE

Alba ·Plena	Fimbriata	Mathotiana Alba
Alba Superba	Finlandia	Mine-No-Yuki
Amabilis	Grandiflora Alba	Mrs. Chas. Simons
Candidissima	Haku-Rakuten	Nobilissima
Caprice	Hakutsuru	Purity
Cuspidata	Il Cygno	Setsugekka
Dante	Imura	Snowdrift
Elizabeth	K. Sawada	Triphosa
Elizabeth Boardman	Lilyi	White Empress
Ethrington White	Magnoliaeflora Alba	White Giant

CAMELLIAS LISTED ACCORDING TO COLOR

PINK

Aitonia
Akebono
Augusta Wilson
Beali Rosea
Bessie McArthur
Caleb Cope
Cameo Pink
Christine Lee
Claudia Lee
Cliveana
Debutante
Duke of Wellington
Eleanor Hagood
Enrico Bettoni

Francine
Frau Minna Seidel
Hibiscus
High Hat
Jean Keer
Kumasaka
Lady Clare
Lady Mary Cromartie
Lallarook
Lurie's Favorite
Magnoliaeflora
Magnoliaeflora English
Marchioness of Exeter
Martha Brice

Mathotiana Rosea
Monarch
Mrs. Freeman Weiss
Otome
Pink Ball
Pink Star
Reticulata
Rev. John Bennett
Rev. John G. Drayton
Rosea
Rosea Superba
Rosita
Semi-double Blush
Stardust

VARIEGATED

Adolphe Audusson Var.
Akebono Var.
Alexander Nowland
Aspasia
Bella Romana
Catherine Cathcart
Cleopatra
C. M. Hovey
Coletti Maculata
Comte de Gomer
Countess of Orkney
Daikagura
Donckelari
Duc d'Orleans

Duchess of Sutherland
Elegans (Chandler)
Elizabeth Arden
Eugene Lizze
Gigantea
Governor Mouton
Harlequin
Herme
Kellingtonia
Kumasaka Var.
Lady Vansittart
Latifolia
Madame Haas
Mathotiana Var.

Matsukasa
Mikenjaku
Monjisu
Mrs. Anne Marie Hovey
Mrs. Lurman
Peoniflora
Princess Baciocchi
Sara-Sa
Somegawa
Sophia
Sweeti Vera
T. K. Variegated
Tricolor (Siebold)
Ville de Nantes

Blooms from the seed of one bush grown by W. M. McClellan, charter member of the Men's Camellia Club, Pensacola, Fla. He planted 125 seed which produced 118 plants and 8 to 10 different varieties of bloom. *F.N.P.S. Photo*

VARIETIES

The following list of more than 160 varieties is considered a representative group of the several hundred camellias available.

The inclusion of any particular variety does not necessarily mean that it is outstanding. Also, many new and interesting varieties were omitted because of lack of space and often because they are still too scarce to be easily obtained.

An attempt was made to include the ones that have been voted most popular in representative polls and varieties that commercial growers have advised are the most popular with amateur growers.

The list also includes the 50 varieties included in the initial report of the committee on classification of varieties of the American Camellia Society and is headed by Dr. H. Harold Hume, chairman.

Varieties are usually cross indexed under the various names they are sometimes known by but descriptions are listed only under the preferred name which always appears in capital letters.

Special thanks is due Mr. R. J. Wilmot, secretary of the American Camellia Society, for assistance in selecting the preferred name of most varieties listed. This was done to further the effort of the society in their attempt to clarify and classify names and varieties in our belief that their work along this line is in the interest of both amateur and professional growers.

Mr. H. H. Harms, past president of the Oregon Camellia Society, and a member of the name classification committee of the American Society, also deserves much credit for his assistance in preparing the list for Mr. Wilmot's final check.

PRONUNCIATION

There is practically no written authority for the pronunciation of the various names given to varieties of camellias. Even the largest unabridged dictionaries leave out the names of the varieties. Several of the reference books on camellias give the names; but seldom give the pronunciation. There is, therefore, a real need for a standardized list of pronunciations.

The pronunciation of camellia varieties offers some special difficulties. The names come from many foreign languages — Latin, Dutch, Japanese, French, etc. To make these an integral part of the American language has required a considerable change from the original pronunciation in some instances.

The pronunciations given are not artificial pronunciations; but are recorded from the speech of camellia growers who use the names familiarly every day. Because of this familiar use, the words have been Americanized until they fit easily into an English sentence.

It would have been desirable in some ways to use a scientific phonetic alphabet in indicating pronunciation. The fact, however, that many people do not understand and use a scientific phonetic alphabet caused the substitution of a simple syllabic representation which is obviously somewhat crude and inaccurate; but which can be understood by everyone without special training.

In using this phonetic alphabet, or any other, the reader should remember that words should be "pronounced trippingly on the tongue" and not spelled out painfully.

The phonetic transcriptions were made by Harold H. Sherley. The final authority, however, is the hundreds of camellia growers who have fashioned the pronunciations through daily use.

Adolphe (j)—ADOLPHE AUDUSSON
ADOLPHE AUDUSSON* (j), (*ay* dolf *odd* uh sun)—Adolphe
    Very large semi-double, red; prominent stamens in form of crown.
    Mid-season.
ADOLPHE AUDUSSON VAR. (j)—The Czar
    Variegated red and white form of ADOLPHE AUDUSSON.
    Mid-season.
AITONIA* (j), (eye *tohn* yuh)
    Large semi-double, rose pink; clustered stamens in center.
    Mid-season.
AKEBONO (j), (ak uh *bohn* yuh)
    Large semi-double, soft pink; prominent stamens and hardy bloomer; often fragrant.
AKEBONO VAR. (j)
    Similar to the AKEBONO, but with white markings.
    Mid-season.
ALBA PLENA* (j), (*al* buh *plee* nuh)
    Large imb., pure white.
    Early.
Alba Plena Fimbriata (j)—FIMBRIATA
ALBA SUPERBA (j), (*al* buh suh *per* buh)
    Large semi-double, pure white; showy stamens; hardy bloomer.
    Mid-season.
ALEXANDER NOWLAND (j), (*noh* land)
    Medium to large full double, bright red marbled with white.
    Mid-season.
Aloha (j)—AREJISHI

---

* One of 50 in American Camellia Society '46 Book.
(j) *japonica* (species)
(s) *saluenensis*
(S) *Sasanqua*
(r) *reticulata*
(c) *cuspidata*

123

AMABILIS (j), (uh *mah* buh lis)—White Poppy
Large single, poppy like, white with heavy cluster of yellow stamens.
Mid-season.

Anemonaeflora (j)—WARRATAH

Anna Frost (j)—COMTE de GOMER

ANNE LINDBERGH (j)
Medium large, deep rose pink to red; peony form. Late.

APPLE BLOSSOM* (s)
Single, white blushed with pink; slender petals, fragrant; early.

APPLE BLOSSOM (S) or (j)
Similar to APPLE BLOSSOM (s).
Early.

AREJISHI* (j), (air uh *jee* shee)—Aloha
Large, dark red, peony form. Early.

ASPASIA (j), (uh *spay* shuh)—Czarina, Empress of Russia, Emperor of Russia Var.
Large peony form, deep crimson splotched with white; hardy bloomer.
Mid-season.

AUGUSTA WILSON (j)—Cabbage Head, St. Elmo
Large peony form, soft pink.
Mid-season.

AUNT JETTY (j)—Governor Mouton Red
Large double, red, peony type. Mid-season.

BEALI ROSEA (j), (*beel* eye roh *zee* uh)—Mrs. John Laing
Medium-sized, salmon pink, full double blossom.
Mid-season.

BELLA ROMANA* (j), (*bell* uh ro *mahn* uh)—Tri-color Imbricata, Madame de Strekaloff
Large loosely petaled, light pink striped crimson—sometimes ivory white striped crimson.
Mid-season.

BESSIE McARTHUR (j)
Very large semi-double, clear pink; prominent stamens.
Late.

BLACK PRINCE (j)
Small semi-double mahogany red with red stamens.
Late.

Blood of China (j)—VICTOR EMMANUEL

Blood of Christ (j)—MATHOTIANA ALBA

Bolen's Pride (j)—RUBY GLOW

Cabbage Head (j)—AUGUSTA WILSON

CALEB COPE (j)
Medium to large, clear rose pink; fully imb.
Mid-season.

CALIFORNIA (j)
Very large loose double, rose red; has broad thick petals.
Mid-season.

CAMEO PINK (j)
Small a medium full double symmetrical, light pink. Mid-season.

CAMPBELLI (j), (kamm bel eye)—Gen. Douglas MacArthur
Large full double peony form, red.
Mid-season to late.

CANDIDISSIMA* (j), (kann duh *diss* uh muh)
Imb., medium-sized pure white; star-shaped; profuse bloomer.
Late.
CAPRICE (j), (kuh *prees*)
Medium-sized double, creamy white, usually fragrant.
Mid-season.
CATHERINE CATHCART (j)
Large, full symmetrical double, pink mottled white.
Mid-season to late.
Celtic Rosea (j)—SEMI-DOUBLE BLUSH
Chandler Elegans (j)—ELEGANS (CHANDLER)
Chandleri Elegans (j)—ELEGANS (CHANDLER)
CHEERFUL (j)
Medium-sized full double; free blooming; red.
Mid-season.
CLAUDIA LEE* (j)
Large single, clear pink; free blooming. Mid-season.
CLEOPATRA (S)
Semi-double, rose pink flecked with white.
Early.
CLIVEANA (j), (kleye vee *ann* uh)
Large semi-double; peony type; clear pink. Mid-season.
C. M. HOVEY* (j), (*huvv* ee)—Colonel Firey, Wm. S. Hastie (Miss.)
Large double; imb.; flat blossom; dark red. Late.
COLETTI MACULATA (j), (koh *lett* ee mack yu *laht* uh)—Girard Debaillon
Medium-sized semi-double, intense red and pure white; peony type.
Mid-season.
Colonel Firey (j)—C. M. HOVEY
COMTE DE GOMER (j), (kahmt duh *gohmer*)—Anna Frost
Medium-sized double, delicate pink, flecked red.
Mid-season.
COUNTESS OF ORKNEY (j)
Small double, light pink striped red (sometimes white striped red); imb.; profuse bloomer.
Mid-season.
CUSPIDATA (c) (a species), (kuss pee *daht* uh)
Small single, white.
Czarina (j)—ASPASIA
DAIKAGURA (j), (deye kuh *goor* uh)
Large double, deep pink and white variegated, peony form. Very early.
DAIKAGURA RED* (j)
Large, full, loosely petaled peony type; deep rose; free blooming.
Early.
DAITERIN (j), (deye *tear* inn)
Single pink with circular crown of petaloids. Late.
DANTE (j), (*dan* tee)—Pine Cone White
Medium-large full double; symmetrical; pure white.
Mid-season to Late.
Dearest (j)—FINLANDIA

DEBUTANTE* (j), (deb yoo *tahnt*)—Sara C. Hastie
Large full peony type; light pink. Early.

Diana (j)—IMURA

Dr. Sheppard Red (j)—TE DEUM

DONCKELARI* (j), (dahng *klair* eye) or (*dahng* klur eye)
Large semi-double, red marbled white. Mid-season.

Donckelari California (j)—MONJISU

DR. W. G. LEE (j)
Large semi-double; rich dark red. Mid-season.

DUC d'ORLEANS (j), (dook dor *leenz*)—Marguerite Gouillon
Large full peony type; prominent stamens; ivory flecked with pink.
Mid-season.

Duc d'Orleans Pink (j)—STARDUST

DUCHESS OF SUTHERLAND (j)
Large semi-double; open petaled; white; with occasional pink stripe on one petal; cluster
of stamens in center. Mid-season.

Duncan Bell (j)—MENA LADNIER

DUKE of WELLINGTON (j)
Large pink. Semi-double with stamens intermixed in the petals.
Mid-season.

ECSTASY (j)
Medium-size formal double; clear pink. Mid-season.

ELEANOR HAGOOD (j)
Medium to large full double; symmetrical; pale pink. Late.

ELEGANS (CHANDLER)* (j)—Chandler Elegans, Chandleri Elegans.
Large anemone type; deep rose pink usually mottled white.
Early to Mid-season.

ELENA NOBILE (j), (uh *lee* nuh noh *beel*)—Napa Red
Medium-sized double; brilliant flame red, yellow stamens. Late.

ELIZABETH (j)—Montironi
Large full double; imb.; symmetrical; white occasionally showing faint pink stripe.
Late.

ELIZABETH ARDEN (j)
Medium to large; opening with rosebud center and changing to semi-double with stamens
visible; soft pink and white striped rose.
Mid-season.

ELIZABETH BOARDMAN (j)
Large semi-double; white; fluted; golden stamens intermixed.
Mid-season.

ELLA DRAYTON (j)
Large full double red with tiered petals forming a star; free blooming.
Late.

EMPEROR (j)
Medium-size double type; rose red. Imported variety not to be confused with Emperor
synonym of Emperor of Russia. Mid-season.

Emperor (j)—EMPEROR of RUSSIA

EMPEROR of RUSSIA (j)—Emperor
Large double; multi-centered; scarlet.
Mid-season.

Emperor of Russia Var. (j)—ASPASIA
Emperor Wilhelm (j)—GIGANTEA
Empress (j)—LADY CLARE
Empress of Russia (j)—ASPASIA
ENRICO BETTONI (j), (en *ree* koh buh *toh* nee)—Venus
Large semi-double peony form; irregular petals interspersed with stamens; rose pink.
Mid-season.
ETHRINGTON WHITE (j)—Waterloo
Large semi-double with large crinkled petals showing stamens interspersed among petals;
pure white. Mid-season.
EUGENE LIZZE (j), (*lizz* ee)—Lady Jane Grey
Medium to large semi-double to double peony form; light rose flecked with white.
Mid-season.
Fanny Bolis (j)—LATIFOLIA
FEASTI* (j)
Large double; fully imbricated; white dashed with pink; often solid pink.
Mid-season.
FIMBRIATA* (j), (fimm bree *aht* uh)—Fimbriata Alba
Medium to large full double imb.; white with edges of petals fringed.
Early.
Fimbriata Alba (j)—FIMBRIATA
Fimbriata Superba (j)—FRED SANDER
FINLANDIA (j), (finn *land* yuh)—Dearest
Large semi-double, white with swirled petals; mass of prominent stamens in center.
Mid-season.
Firegold (j)—TE DEUM
FLAME (j)
Large single to semi-double, deep flame red; stamens in center.
Mid-season.
Flora Celeste (j)—PEONIFLORA
FRANCINE (j), (frann *seen*)
Very large anemone type, deep rose pink.
Mid-season.
FRAU MINNA SEIDEL* (j), (frou *minn* uh *see* dul)—Pink Perfection
Medium-sized double fully imb., clear shell pink; profuse bloomer.
FRED SANDER (j)—Fimbriata Superba
Large semi-double with deeply fringed petals, brilliant red occasionally dotted white.
Late.
FRIZZLE WHITE (j)
Large semi-double white; yellow stamens and wavy petals.
Gen. Douglas MacArthur (j)—CAMPBELLI
GIGANTEA (j), (jeye *gant* ee uh)—Emperor Wilhelm
Very large semi-double peony form, red heavily mottled white.
Mid-season.
Girard Deballion (j)—COLETTI MACULATA
GLEN 40 (j)
Large fully symmetrical double, dark red. Mid-season.
GLOIRE DE NANTES* (j), (*glor* ee duh nahns)
Large semi-double, red; center petals whorled; free bloomer. Mid-season.

Gloire de Nantes Var. (j)—LATIFOLIA

GOSHO-GURUMA (j), (gosh uh goo *room* uh)
Large single, deep red; cluster of petaloids and stamens in center.
Mid-season.

GOVERNOR MOUTON* (j), (*moh* tun)
Large irregular semi-double, oriental red; some petals blotched white.
Mid-season.

Governor Mouton Red (j)—AUNT JETTY

GRANDIFLORA ALBA (j)—Lotus
Very large, white; resembles water lily; prominent yellow stamens.
Mid-season.

Grandiflora Rosea (j)—LADY CLARE

Gunnelli (j)—MONARCH

HAKU-RAKUTEN (j), (*hah* koo rah *koo* tun)
Large loose double to peony form, pure white; petals curved satiny and fluted.
Mid-season.

HAKUTSURU (j), (*hah* koo *soo* roo)
Quite similar to HAKU-RAKUTEN except that petals are more delicate, fragile and upright. Midseason.

HARLEQUIN (j), (*hahr* luh kwin)
Medium-sized, varying from double peony to full double; clear shell pink or sometimes pink and white. Late. (Pink double variety resembles Frau Minna Seidel which it sometimes replaces in areas where latter's buds drop excessively.)

HERME* (j), (*her* mee)—Hikaru Gengi, Jordan's Pride, Souvenir de Henri Guichard
Large semi-double, light pink bordered white and lined deep pink.
Mid-season.

HIBISCUS (j), (heye *biss* kus)
Very large single to semi-double, blush pink; prominent stamens; free bloomer.
Early to Mid-season.

HIGH HAT (j)
Large full peony type, pale pink. A new California favorite. Early.

Hikaru Gengi (j)—HERME

IL CYGNO (j), (*sigg* noh)—The Swan
Large pure white, imb. Late.

Il Tramonto (j)—LALLAROOK

IMPERATOR (j), (im per *ay* tor)
Large loose peony form, light red.
Early.

IMURA* (j), (ee *moor* uh)—Diana
Very large semi-double, snow white; stamens prominent and upstanding.
Mid-season.

JARVIS RED (j)
Medium large semi-double, vivid deep red; golden stamens; prolific bloomer.
Mid-season.

Jordan's Pride (j)—HERME

Julia Drayton (Calif.) (j)—MATHOTIANA

KELLINGTONIA (j)
Very large open peony type, orange red striped or blotched white; heavy bloomer. An imported variety. Similar to Gigantea except that bloom is smaller.

GRANDIFLORA ALBA

La Peppermint

VILLE DE NANTES

FLAME

FRAU MINNA SEIDEL

KIMBERLEY* (j)
Large single, carmine with red stamens.
Mid-season.

K. SAWADA* (j), (suh *wahd* uh). (U.S. patent No. 431.)
Large full double imb., pure white; heavy bloomer.
Mid-season.

KUMASAKA* (j), (koo muh *sah* kah)—Lady Marion
Large semi-double to loose double, deep rose pink veined slightly darker, prominent stamens. Mid-season to late.

KUMASAKA VAR. (j)
Large semi-double to loose double, deep rose pink spotted white.
Mid-season.

Ladiner's Red (j)—POPE PIUS IX

LADY CLARE*(j)—Empress, Grandiflora Rosea
Very large semi-double, deep rose pink.
Mid-season.

LADY HUME'S BLUSH* (j)
Medium-sized full double imb., white tinged with blush pink.
Mid-season.

Lady Jane Grey (j)—EUGENE LIZZE
Lady Marion (j)—KUMASAKA

LADY MARY CROMARTIE (j), (kruh *mahr* tee)
Large semi-double, deep rose pink; peony form.
Mid-season.

LADY VANSITTART* (j)
Large semi-double, deep pink to red and white variegated; golden stamens in center; free bloomer. Mid-season.

LADY VANSITTART RED (j)
Medium-sized semi-double, bright red; profuse bloomer.
Late.

LALLAROOK* (j)—Il Tramonto, Laurel Leaf
Large full double imb., light pink often with soft white mottling; often has incurved petals.
Mid-season.

LATIFOLIA* (j), (lat uh *fohl* ee uh)—Fanny Bolis, Gloire de Nantes Var., Leana Superba Var.
Large semi-double, rich red with white blotches.
Mid-season.

Laurel Leaf (j)—LALLAROOK
Leana Superba Var. (j)—LATIFOLIA
Lewis Red Peony (j)—VEDRINE

LIBERY BELL (j)
Semi-peony form; pure white; long blooming season.

Lilli (j)—LILYI

LILYI* (j), (*lill* ee eye)—Lilli
Medium-sized double, imb., pearly white; profuse bloomer.
Mid-season through late.

Lotus (j)—GRANDIFLORA ALBA

LURIE'S FAVORITE (j), (loor eez)
Large semi-double, pale lavender pink; fluted petals; crown of stamens in center.
Mid-season.

133

Madame de Strekaloff (j)—BELLA ROMANA

MADAME HAAS (j), (hahs)
Full double imb., light red with occasional pink stripe in center.
Mid-season.

MAGNOLIAEFLORA* (j), (mag *nohl* yuh flor uh)—Rose of Dawn
Large semi-double, deep pink at base paling to blush pink at tips of petals; shows stamens.
Mid-season.

MAGNOLIAEFLORA ALBA (j)
Large semi-double, white; prominent stamens.
Mid-season.

MAGNOLIAEFLORA ENGLISH (j)
Medium-sized semi-double with pointed petals; flesh pink.
Mid-season.

MARCHIONESS of EXETER (j)
Large full peony type, pale pink (sometimes flecked deep pink or white).
Early to Mid-season.

Marguerite Gouillon (j)—DUC d'ORLEANS

MARION MITCHELL (j)
Large semi-double, scarlet red.
Mid-season.

MARTHA BRICE (j)
Large semi-double peony form, pale lavender pink; large fluted petals.
Mid-season.

Mary E. M. (j)—REV. JOHN G. DRAYTON

MATHOTIANA* (j), (muh *thoh* tee ann uh)—Julia Drayton (Calif.), Mathotiana Rubra,
Purple Dawn, Purple Emperor, Wm. S. Hastie (S.C.)
Very large double, symmetrical, deep, dark red. Petals are purplish under certain weather
condition. In warm weather opens to show stamens.
Mid-season.

MATHOTIANA ALBA* (j)—Blood of Christ
Very large full double, imb., pure white (sometimes has faint pink line).
Late.

MATHOTIANA ROSEA* (j)—Pink Beauty
Very large double, imb., pink; has bud-like center.
Mid-season.
Sport of Mathotiana Alba

Mathotiana Rubra (j)—MATHOTIANA

MATHOTIANA VAR. (j) (Sometimes erroneously called C. M. Hovey)
Same as MATHOTIANA but variegated with white spots.

MATSUKASA* (j), (matt soo *kah* suh)—Pine Cone
Large, high centered double with wavy petals standing apart, rose red with white markings.
Late.

MENA LADNIER (j), (*mee* nuh *ladd* neer)—Duncan Bell
Very large anemone type, blood red (occasionally flecked with white).
Mid-season.

MIKENJAKU (j), (mick en *jock* oo)—Nagasaki
Very large semi-double, deep rose marbled white.
Mid-season.

MINE-NO-YUKI (S), (mee nuh no *yoo* kee)—Snow on Mountain
Medium-sized double, pure white; outer petals cupped toward center.

MONARCH (j)—Gunnelli
Large double multi-center peony form, deep pink. Mid-season.
MONJISU*(j), (mahn *jee* soo)Donckelari California
Medium-sized semi-double, symmetrical, cherry red and white variegated. Mid-season.
MONJISU RED(j)
Medium-sized semi-double, vivid red; stamens with pink filament and yellow anther.
Mid-season.
Montironi (j)—ELIZABETH
MRS. ABBY WILDER* (j)
Medium-sized, high centered peony form, white lightly flecked with pink.
Mid-season.
MRS. ANNE MARIE HOVEY* (j), (*huvv* ee)
Large double fully imb., rose mottled white. Mid-season.
MRS. CHARLES COBB (j)
Large semi-double, very dark red with golden stamens. Mid-season.
MRS. CHAS. SIMONS (j), (*simm* uhnz)
Large semi-double, pure white. Mid-season.
MRS. FREEMAN WEISS (j)
Large loose semi-double, pink with wavy petals. Mid-season.
Mrs. John Laing (j)—BEALI ROSEA
MRS. K. SAWADA (j), (suh *wah* duh). (U. S. Patent No. 481.)
Medium-sized full double, imb., delicate pink shaded on white. Late.
MRS. LURMAN* (j)
Medium-sized double, imb., red marbled white. Late.
Nagasaki (j)—MIKENJAKU
Napa Red (j)—ELENA NOBILE
NOBILISSIMA* (j), (noh *bliss* uh muh)
Medium-sized double peony, white shading to yellow at base.
Early to Mid-season.
OTOME (j), (oh *toh* mee) or (oh *tohm*)
Medium to large full double, delicate pink, petals edged with white. Mid-season.
OTOME RED (j)
Medium-sized full double, deep cherry red; flowers freely. Mid-season.
PEONIFLORA (j)—Flora Celeste
Very large shaggy peony type, white to creamy white marked with rose.
Early to Mid-season.
Pine Cone (j)—MATSUKASA
Pine Cone White (j)—DANTE
PINK BALL (j)
Large irregular peony form, shell pink. Mid-season.
Pink Beauty (j)—MATHOTIANA ROSEA
Pink Perfection (j)—FRAU MINNA SEIDEL
PINK STAR (j)
Large semi-double, star shaped, deep pink. Late.
POPE PIUS IX (j)—Ladiner's Red, Prince Eugene Napoleon
Large full double, imb., dark red. Mid-season.
Porter's Rose (j)—SOPHIA
Prince Eugene Napoleon (j)—POPE PIUS IX
PRINCESS BACIOCCHI (j), (*baht* shee *aht* shee)
Medium-sized full double, dark red mottled white. Late.

135

PROFESSOR C. S. SARGENT* (j)
Medium-sized very double high centered, peony form, deep scarlet. Mid-season.
PURITY* (j)
Large full double, symmetrical, pure white. Mid-season.
Purple Dawn (j)—MATHOTIANA
Purple Emperor (j)—MATHOTIANA

Red Ball (j)—MONARCH
RETICULATA (r) (a species), (ruh tick yoo *lah* tuh)
Very large semi-double, carmine pink; fluted petals. Mid-season.
REV. JOHN BENNETT (j)
Large semi-double, salmon pink; conspicuous stamens. Mid-season to late.
REV. JOHN G. DRAYTON (j)—Mary E. M.
Medium large loose semi-double form, pink. Mid-season to late.
Robin Hood (j)—TRICOLOR RED
Rose of Dawn (j)—MAGNOLIAEFLORA
ROSEA (S)
Large single, deep pink; cluster of stamens in center.
ROSEA SUPERBA (j)
Very large full double form, deep pink. A pink or rose sport of Mathotiana. Late.
ROSITA (j), (roh *zee* tuh)
Medium-sized full double, symmetrical, bright rose pink. Late.
ROYAL WHITE (j)
Large vari-form semi-double to full imb. double; pure white. Late.
Ruby Glow (j)—VEDRINE

Sara C. Hastie (j)—DEBUTANTE
SARA-SA* (j), (*sair* us sah)—Sawada
Large semi-double, flesh pink dotted and striped deeper pink; yellow stamens in center.
Mid-season.
SARAH FROST (j)
Large full double, imb., rose red. Mid-season to late.
Sawada (j)—SARA-SA
SEMI-DOUBLE BLUSH* (j)—Celtic Rosea
Medium-sized semi-double, blush pink, magnolia type with loose crown of stamens.
Mid-season.
SETSUGEKKA (S), (sett soo *gekk* uh)
Large, semi-double, pure white with just a touch of pink at end of the slightly ruffled
petals.
SNOWDRIFT (j)
Large semi-double water lily type, snow white. Mid-season.
Snow on Mountain (S)—MINE-NO-YUKI
SOMEGAWA (j), (soh muh *gah* wah)
Large double, variegated red and white. Late.
SOPHIA (j), (soh *fee* yuh)—Porter's Rose
Very large, pink and white. Mid-season. Also a red variety.
SOUV. de BAHUAUD LITOU* (j), (soo vuh *neer* duh bah *oh* lee *too*)
Large double loosely imb., soft rose. Sport of MATHOTIANA ALBA. Late.
Souv. de Henri Buichard (j), HERME
STARDUST (j)—Duc d'Orleans Pink
Large semi-double peony type, bright pink. Mid-season.

St. Elmo (j)—AUGUSTA WILSON
SWEETI VERA (j), (*sweet* eye *vair* uh)
  Large loose peony form, flesh pink flecked rose. Mid-season.
TE DEUM (j), (tee *dee* uhm) or (tay *day* uhm)—Dr. Sheppard, Firegold
  Very large semi-double, peony or sometimes full double blooms; brilliant red.
  Mid-season to late.
The Czar (j)—ADOLPHE AUDUSSON
The Swan (j)—IL CYGNO
T. K. VARIEGATED* (j)
  Medium-sized semi-double, light pink with dark pink margin; opens flat with large cluster
  yellow stamens. Mid-season.
Tri-color Imbricata (j)—BELLA ROMANA
TRICOLOR RED (j)—Robin Hood, Wakanoura Red
  Large semi-double, rich red; edges of petals cupped inward. Mid-season.
TRICOLOR (SIEBOLD)* (j)—Wakanoura
  Large semi-double, variegated pink and red with white; petals slightly cupped inward;
  prominent golden stamens. Mid-season.
TRIPHOSA (j), (treye *foh* suh)
  Large single to semi-double, white; slightly cupped with ring of yellow stamens.
UNCLE SAM (j)
  Large double; rich rose red or red and white var. Mid-season.
VALTEVAREDA (j)
  Formal cup-shaped double; deep pink. Late.
VEDRINE (j), (vuh *dreen*)—Ruby Glow
  Large loose peony type, ruby red. Mid-season to late.
Venus (j)—ENRICO BETTONI
VICTOR EMMANUEL (j)—Blood of China.
  Very large semi-double, orange red; cluster of stamens in center. Late.
VICTORY WHITE (j)
  Large semi-double; pure white with numerous petalets and stamens. Mid-season.
VILLE de NANTES (j)
  Large semi-double, rose red splotched white; serrated petals; stamens in form of crown.
  Late.
VILLE de NANTES RED (j), (veel duh nahns)
  Large semi-double, red; serrated petals; stamens upstanding in form of crown. Late.
Wakanoura (j)—TRICOLOR (SIEBOLD)
Wakanoura Red (j)—TRICOLOR RED
WARRATAH (j), (*wawr* uh tah)—Anemonaeflora
  Dark crimson, anemone type bloom. Mid-season.
Waterloo (j)—ETHRINGTON WHITE
WHITE EMPRESS (j)
  Very large semi-double, pure white; broad petals; yellow stamens. Early to Mid-season.
WHITE GIANT (j)
  Very large semi-double, pure white with numerous yellow stamens. Mid-season.
WHITE HIBISCUS (j), (heye *biss* kus)
  Large single to semi-double; snow white petals, yellow stamens. Early.
WHITE KING (j)
  Semi-double, large porcelain texture petals, snow white with yellow stamens.
White Poppy (j)—AMABILIS
Wm. S. Hastie (Mississippi) (j)—C. M. HOVEY
Wm. S. Hastie (South Carolina) (j)—MATHOTIANA

ALBA PLENA

PURITY

MATHOTIANA

Left—Not fully open   Right—Open showing stamens

SOMEGAWA

ROSITA

CLIMAX*

DONCKELARI

RED HIBISCUS

ADOLPHE AUDUSSON VAR.

BESSIE McARTHUR

EMPEROR OF RUSSIA

*Ella Drayton Var.

LALLAROOK

FRAU MINNA SEIDEL

VILLE DE NANTES
Red

TE DEUM
(Not fully open)

ELLA DRAYTON

OTOME

WHITE HIBISCUS

LA REINE VAR.

REV. JOHN G. DRAYTON

FINLANDIA

HERMESPORT

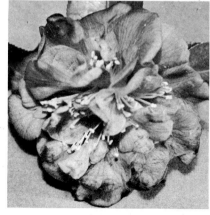

VEDRINE

MATHOTIANA ROSEA

BEALI ROSEA

NOBILISSIMA

DAIKAGURA

MRS. CHAS. SIMONS

CALIFORNIA

ELIZABETH

TRIPHOSA

MARION MITCHELL

SOPHIA

DANTE

OTOME RED

REGINA de GIGANTEA

ELENA NOBILE

ANNE LINDBERGH

ADOLPHE AUDUSSON (Sport)

POPE PIUS IX

ELEGANS (CHANDLER)

ETHRINGTON WHITE

MATHOTIANA ALBA

LADY MARY CROMARTIE

DAIKAGURA RED

HAKUTSURU

145

SNOWDRIFT

PINK STAR

LATIFOLIA

COLETTI MACULATA

ALBA SUPERBA

FUJI-NO-MINE (S)

APPRECIATION

To be assured of accurate information regarding proper methods of planting and caring for camellias in the various sections of the country, the advice of the following nurseries and seed stores was asked. We wish to thank these firms for the assistance they have rendered and the advice they have given us regarding the proper methods of care for camellias in their particular area. Key letters following the names of nurseries indicate that they supply camellias at—

(R) Retail; (R & W) Retail and Wholesale; (W) Wholesale only.

ALABAMA

Blackwell Nurseries (W)
Semmes, Alabama

Cottage Hill Nursery (R & W)
P. O. Box 484 Mobile 3, Alabama

Dalraida Nursery (R)
R. F. D. No. 4, Montgomery, Alabama

Loop Nursery (R & W)
2406 Grant Street, Mobile, Alabama

Overlook Nurseries (R & W)
Crichton Station, Mobile, Alabama

Emmett J. Pfingstl's Nursery (R & W)
P. O. Box 1870, 101 Willena Avenue
Montgomery 3, Alabama

Semmes Nurseries (W)
Semmes, Alabama

CALIFORNIA

California Nursery Company (R)
Niles, California

Camellia Hall (R & W)
4950 44th Street
Sacramento, California

Davis' Camellia & Orchid Gardens
(R & W)
521 Lower Azusa Road
El Monte, California

Germain Seed and Plant Co. (R & W)
747 Terminal Street
Los Angeles 21, California

Paul J. Howard's California Flower-
land (R)
11700 National Blvd.
Los Angeles 34, California

Navlet's (R)
1971 Telegraph Avenue
Oakland 12, California

Oak Ridge Camellia Gardens (R & W)
Rt. 4, Box 460, Occidental, California

Rancho Del Descanso (W)
La Canada, California

Saratoga Camellia Nursery (R & W)
P. O. Box 541, Saratoga, California

Toichi Domoto (R & W)
26591 Western Road
Hayward, California

Valley Garden Supply Co. (R & W)
11239 Ventura Blvd.
North Hollywood, California

Wiles Camellia Nursery (R & W)
1519 Simpson Street
Fresno 4, California*

FLORIDA

Florida Nursery & Landscape Co. (R)
Box 97, Leesburg, Florida

Lee Floral Garden (R & W)
P. O. Box 1007, Pensacola, Florida

Taylor's Nursery (R)
Rt. 3, Box 262, Pensacola, Florida

GEORGIA

Oliver Industries (R)
1501 N. Patterson Street
Valdosta, Georgia

Sea Island Nursery (R & W)
St. Simons Island, Georgia

Wight Nurseries (R & W)
Cairo, Georgia

LOUISIANA

Edward Robert Gschwind (R)
6071 Laurel Street
New Orleans 15, Louisiana

E. A. McIllhenny (R & W)
Avery Island, Louisiana

C. G. Simon Nursery, Inc. (R & W)
304 Breaux Bridge Avenue
Lafayette, Louisiana

SOUTH CAROLINA

Magnolia Gardens & Nurseries (R & W)
R. F. D. No. 2
Johns Island, South Carolina

Wildwood Nurseries (R & W)
Walterboro, South Carolina

TEXAS

M. H. Black Nursery (R & W)
510 Decatur Avenue
Orange, Texas

Feray's Fine Flowers (R & W)
2110 Long
Beaumont, Texas

Lone Oak Nursery (R & W)
520 Decatur Avenue
Orange, Texas

A. J. Smith Co. (R & W)
5001 Broadway
San Antonio, Texas

OREGON

Beaver Creek Nursery (R & W)
Gresham, Oregon

Benedict Nursery Co. (R & W)
735 N. E. 87th
Portland, Oregon

Bradley's Camellia Gardens (R)
4045 King Street
Milwaukie 2, Oregon

Braeger's Oregon Seed (R)
140 S. W. Yamhill Street
Portland 4, Oregon

Doerflers—Nurseryman (R & W)
150 North Lancaster Street
Salem, Oregon

Ferrill's Nursery (R & W)
Route 8, Box 1246, Salem, Oregon

Frederick's Garden Shop (R)
726 S. W. 4th Avenue
Portland 4, Oregon

Parkrose Nursery (R)
10815 N. E. Sandy Blvd.
Portland 13, Oregon

Portland Camellia Gardens (R & W)
Route 5
Portland 1, Oregon

Portland Rose Nursery (R & W)
7240 S. E. Division
Portland 6, Oregon

Rich & Sons Nursery (R & W)
Hillsboro, Oregon

J. F. Senko Nursery (W)
Cornelius, Oregon

Stone's Flowers (R)
Coos Bay, Oregon

Swiss Floral Greenhouse (R)
1920 N. E. 7th Avenue
Portland 12, Oregon*

Swiss Floral Nursery Co. (R & W)
4531 S. E. 26th Avenue
Portland 2, Oregon

Charles A. Vollum (R & W)
1115 S.E. Lambert Street
Portland, Oregon

Woodlawn Nursery (R & W)
908 N. E. Columbia Blvd.
Portland 11, Oregon

Carlton Nursery Company (R & W)
Forest Grove, Oregon

WASHINGTON

Frank Bonnell's Nursery (R & W)
Route 4, Box 90
Renton, Washington

Campus Nursery, Inc. (R)
5000—25th Ave. N.E.
Seattle 5, Washington

Lackamas Gardens (R & W)
Route 1, Box 5A
Camas, Washington

Malmo Nurseries, Inc. (R & W)
4700—25th Ave., N.E.
Seattle 5, Washington

Puget Sound Seed & Nursery Co. (R)
La Conner, Washington

* Do not solicit out-of-state mail orders.

148

VALTEVAREDA

ELLA DRAYTON

SNOWDRIFT

MIKENJAKU

POPE PIUS IX

FRANCINE

THE QUESTION BOX

After checking with leading amateur and professional camellia growers, the following questions were selected as the ones most frequently asked. The answers are those furnished by the same group of experts.

Why are flowers smaller than average?

Insufficient watering throughout the year particularly during the months that buds are developing; planted too deep or in improper or poorly drained soil; insufficient sunlight or ventilation; not enough plant food; or failure to disbud.

Why are there only a few blooms on plant?

Too much or too frequent fertilizing often injures plant or at least forces such rapid growth of the plant itself that buds are not given a chance to set and develop. Root pruning often helps a healthy plant bloom. (Answers to above question apply here too.)

Why do buds drop?

Poor drainage; deep planting; freezing; excess fertilization or at wrong season; or insufficient water while buds are setting, particularly in the late summer and fall months may cause excessive bud drop. Roots from nearby trees may be robbing the camellia of food or moisture.

Should leaves be left on cuttings and graft scions?

Yes, they should have two or more leaves and a minimum of two eyes or growth buds. Cuttings with more than two eyes will branch sooner but longer cuttings or scions are usually considered harder to propagate.

Why do leaves drop?

Excessive leaf drop may be due to too deep planting; poor drainage; starvation; lack of water; excessive or improper fertilization; plant may be "root-bound" either by its container or by heavy clay surrounding the root ball. Also sometimes caused by disturbance of the roots by moles, roots from other trees, or strawberry root weevil.

Why do leaves turn yellow?

Improper planting or drainage; not enough water; starvation or excessive and improper fertilization; not fully established after transplanting; or planted in too hot a location. A Gulf Coast grower answers: "in this area the water table or level is very close to the surface and as a rule camellias must be planted on a knoll (natural or elevated artificially). If your plant is submerged in this type of soil, dig it up and replant in aerated drainable soil."

How deep should camellias be planted?

No deeper than they were planted at the nursery. Camellias are surface feeders and should be planted as shallow as possible. The greatest evil of camellia planting is in setting them too deep. Do not plant so that there will be earth around the trunk. The root should be barely beneath the surface and allowance made for future settling by planting high. The soil under the root ball should be well packed to prevent excessive settling.

What kind of soil do camellias require?

A loose, friable, well drained soil with an acid reaction.

How much space do camellias require?

Camellias are long lived plants that grow to become very large shrubs and even trees. Allowing too little growing space will cause poorly shaped unhealthy plants.

How long do camellias live?

The life expectancy of a camellia that is given the proper attention runs into the hundreds of years. There are camellias in America that were large shrubs at the time of the Civil War.

What causes camellias to grow spindly?

Excessive shade; improper planting; or insufficient water and plant food.

154

When should camellias be watered?

Frequent sprinkling of the foliage is beneficial and helps control pests and disease. Foliage should not be sprinkled while the hot sun is shining on the plant, however. In addition the root ball should be thoroughly soaked once a week during all dry periods. Permitting the plant to dry out, even once, may reflect during the blooming period, even though it be months away.

Does sprinkling harm flowers or buds?

Sprinkling is usually beneficial except when flowers are in bloom. When in bloom do not sprinkle while sun is shining.

Why do the tips of buds and flowers turn brown?

This is not to be confused with the blossom blight disease and is usually caused by climatic conditions. May be due to freezing, excessive hot sun or the combination of rain or water and sun. Drops of water on the blooms act as a magnifying glass when hit by the rays of the sun. This often causes a burn.

Can commercial sprays damage camellias?

Several growers have reported that they believe some DDT sprays are injurious to camellias and recommend that DDT not be used until further tests have been made. Other growers warn that oil emulsion sprays should not be used during extremely hot or cold weather as they have a tendency to open the plant's pores and serious damage may result.

Which varieties are best for cold climates?

Realizing that the answer to this question will have an important bearing on extending the "camellia belt" we quote two answers. The first was submitted by Mr. R. J. Wilmot, Secretary of the American Camellia Society, and the second by a leading wholesale nurseryman who has been most helpful in furnishing information for "Camellias Illustrated."
—*Editor's Note.*)

"Semi-doubles and singles show less damage from cold than do most perfect doubles. Some perfect doubles however will open well even after cold weather providing it does not come at a critical time in their development. Cold in December has caused 100% drop of Elena Nobile buds while just as severe weather in February had no effect on other than open flowers. The variety Carnation will burst into full bloom following a cold spell. A grower on Long Island who uses a back bedroom for winter storage of his plants says that semi-doubles open best. Complete irregular doubles such as Prof. C. S. Sargent will also open well."

"We think the singles and semi-doubles open up better after severe weather than the full formal type doubles and peony form camellias. We usually recommend early blooming kinds, such as Aloha, September Morn, Shiro-Daikagura, Kikutogi and some of the semi-double kinds that we have found open up here well after severe cold, such as Kumasaka Variegated, Lady Clare, Lady Vansittart (plain and variegated), Sergeant Barrios, Kumasaka and Waterloo. We also recommend almost all of the *Sasanqua* varieties, as we think these are particularly good for colder sections. Jarvis Red, Semi-Double Blush and T. K. Variegated are some of the less expensive varieties that seem to be good, and we recommend these in cases where customers want to try out camellias under cold weather before purchasing more expensive kinds."

What variety makes the best root stock for grafting purposes?

Any healthy root stock is suitable. Should there be a choice, select a fast growing, thick stem, hardy, sturdy root variety.

Is the color of the bloom affected by the root stock?

The color of flowers is affected by the understock only when the understock is infected with a virus disease. This is the cause of many of the mottled flowers now being produced. Kumasaka Variegated is an example. White understocks may be infected with virus but this will not change the color of the bloom but may affect the color of the leaves.

Should flowers be picked after wilting?

Yes, to prevent diseases and for appearance of plant.

Do longer cuttings or graft scions grow more rapidly?

Although usually harder to propagate, longer stock usually grows and branches more rapidly because it has more "eyes" or growth buds.

Does it injure the plant to pick the blossoms?

No, a reasonable amount of cutting is beneficial. On young plants take very short stem with the blossoms. The new growth bud is located very close to the bloom and should not be removed. Longer stems may be taken on larger plants where growth is not so important.

When should camellias be fertilized?

After the blooming season and again in June. Under most soil conditions about a handful for each foot height of the plant. Another lighter application may be made in the fall.

Do camellias require good drainage?

Yes, more fatality in camellia culture is due to poor drainage than any other factor. The roots like to be aerated. If roots stand in water, air is closed out and the plant suffers.

Is commercial tea made from camellia leaves?

Yes, from the leaves of camellia *sinuensis*. The flower of this species is not particularly significant.

What varieties are suitable for cut flowers and greenhouse culture?

Among the varieties most widely purchased for the purpose are: Alba Plena, Elegans (Chandler), Herme, Frau Minna Seidel, Pope Pius IX, Prof. C. S. Sargent, Mathotiana Alba, Glen 40, Mangoliaeflora, C. M. Hovey, Daikagura, Debutante, Lallarook, Mathotiana, Pink Ball and Purity.

Can camellias be successfully grown in pots indoors?

Camellias have been grown by amateurs in the northern states in pots and have flowered successfully. The pots are plunged in the soil outside during the summer, where they set buds. When cold weather arrives, the pots are lifted and placed in the sunroom or on a table near a sunny window. The pot is set on pebbles in a tray in which water is kept at all times to provide humidity to prevent the falling of buds. Heavy flowering varieties are preferred, for they repay in a larger measure for the care given.

SNOWBALL

IMURA

GIGANTEA
(Sport)

ELIZABETH BOARDMAN

MAGNOLIAEFLORA ALBA

BLOSSOM ILLUSTRATIONS

Color Illustration Index, Page VIII

159

YOUR CAMELLIAS

This page is included for listing the camellias in your present collection and those you wish to add.

PRESENT VARIETIES		WANTED VARIETIES	
VARIETY	COLOR	VARIETY	COLOR